ENOUGH

ENOUGH

*detangling self-worth
after destruction*

HOPE SHORTT

ENOUGH: *dismantling self-worth after destruction*
Copyright © 2024 by Hope Shortt

All rights reserved. No part of this book may be reproduced in any manner whatsoever without written permission except in the case of brief quotations embodied in critical articles and reviews.

Author: Hope Shortt
Cover and Interior Design: Hope Shortt
ISBN 9798218396237
Imprint: Independently Published
First Printing 2024 / Printed in the USA

This narrative constitutes an account of my personal experiences and memories. Resemblances to real persons, living or dead, or actual events are entirely coincidental. It is inherent in human nature for individual recollections to diverge, and thus, my memories may not precisely align with those of others involved. This diversity of perspective is not merely recognized; it is embraced. The contents herein represent my truth, as I recollect and have chosen to express it. The stories shared are drawn from the author's personal experiences. While every effort has been made to ensure the accuracy of the contents of this book, the author and publisher assume no responsibility for errors, inaccuracies, omissions, or any inconsistencies found within. Neither the author nor the publisher shall be liable for any loss, damage, or disruption caused by such discrepancies.

This book may include references to lyrics, quotes, and other copyrighted materials under the principles of fair use for commentary, critical writing, scholarship, or research. The inclusion of such materials is done with the utmost respect to the original creators and noted. Any identified or recognizable lyrics or quotes remain the property of their respective copyright holders. The use of these elements is intended only to complement the narrative contained within this work. This book includes insights and quotations that have been inspired by "The Traveler's Gift" by Andy Andrews, and it includes some of the words directly from the book. The ideas and reflections shared here are a tribute to the profound impact the book has had on the author's perspective and are used here to further explore related themes in a personal context.

Any inquiries concerning rights and licensing should also be directed to contact@hopeshortt.com

For my people.
Ryan, Berz & Aust

thank you for saving me

Author's Note

For too long, I observed my life unfolding as if I were merely an observer, reluctant to engage with the narratives that shaped me. From the moment I first started to translate my thoughts into written words, I was filled with a blend of fear and exhilaration. I vividly remember the evening I started journaling my life, initially seeing it as a tool for reflection and a step towards self-improvement. Little did I know the profound journey it was setting in motion, one that, years later, would evolve into a memoir.

This writing journey has been more than just putting down my life on paper; it has been a deep dive into my soul, a quest to uncover the truth and buried memories, and my journey into self-discovery. This memoir isn't just a bunch of memories; it's a collection of stormy and uplifting moments that show humans' incredible resilience.

Armed with vulnerability and strength, I'm sharing my story—a story touched by God's grace, filled with fights for self-love, and victories over the pain passed down through generations. It's about stepping out from the shadows of cycles that have gone on for too long into a light where I can see and accept myself for who I am.

By telling you my life story, I'm opening up about the highs and lows that shaped me. This effort to put my heart on paper comes with one big hope—to connect with you, dear reader, to show you the incredible power our stories have to connect, heal, and make us stronger.

In these pages, you'll not just find my thoughts and experiences, but also an invitation—a call to acknowledge our shared humanity, find comfort in our collective strength, and realize that no matter our past or the challenges we face, we all deserve love, kindness, and are worth every single ounce of it.

This memoir is my way of showing how beautiful the journey to finding oneself can be, the importance of inner peace, and a steadfast belief in better days ahead. It's for anyone wandering through life, looking for a sign of hope. My story, with its raw honesty, aims to be that light.

Thank you for letting me share my world with you.

With all my heart,
Hope

Contents

Dedication   v
Author's Note   vi
Prologue   xi

1	Roots of Resilience	1
2	Foundations of Fracture	8
3	A Profound Sense of Loss	21
4	The Fragile Quest to Belong	30
5	When You Know, You Know	42
6	The Unexpected Journey to Success	56
7	Confronting the Pain Within	69
8	The Unraveling of Fragile Threads	76
9	Reclaiming the Reins	88
10	The Retreat	93
11	The Moment of Truth	101
12	The Unfolding Tapestry of My Legacy	106
13	Navigating White Waters	113
14	Hey Girl	121

15	Choose Me	133
16	Unsettling Waves	142
17	Clarity Emerges	149
18	Beauty From Ashes	155
19	Circle of Trust	162
20	You Are Enough	171

Letters 180

Thank You 188

Prologue

Growing up, I lived across from a family that seemed like they had stepped right out of a fairy tale and into my life. Our homes were tucked away among creeks and huge trees. They were a bright spot in my often chaotic life, like a warm, comforting presence. It felt like I was stepping into a completely different world every time I went from their place back to mine.

When I was with them, I often tasted a life so profoundly different from my own. Their daughter, close to my age but perhaps not my accumulated weariness, became like a sister to me. Her father, a preacher, embodied a serenity and devotion that often felt more myth than man. Within their household, love wasn't just spoken; it was a language fluently expressed through actions, laughter, jokes, playful remarks, and unwavering faith in something greater than ourselves.

Do you ever eat, drink, or smell something that takes you right back to your childhood? I have a few, but Dr. Pepper is my #1. It may seem strange considering it's a soda, but it symbolizes the endless generosity and simple joy in their home. There was never a shortage. We weren't allowed to have soda in our home, and I remember being so excited about something so simple when I visited. There, I was also introduced to a deeper understanding of the God I'd learned about since I was a toddler. However, at their home, He was present in the very air, in the gentle tone of a father who preached with his life as much as his words.

One evening, we set out on an adventure in the woods with baby dolls in tow and an imaginary adventure ahead. I noticed something as we climbed the hill, and my friend pointed out to me that her father had built an altar to come and pray and talk to God. As we walked by, I remember glancing back and thinking to myself, "Maybe I need a spot like this to come to pray since I always fall asleep during my prayers at night."

Unbeknownst to me, the first time I laid my eyes on it, there would come a day when I'd run out of my home, breathless, tears staining my face, and fall on the dirt in front of that altar and plead for God to end my life.

As a young girl yearning for validation, significance, and acceptance, I realized from an early age that I was always seeking to understand my worth. I frequently pondered why I couldn't have a caring home like the one nearby, a father who loved me unconditionally, or a mother who exuded contentment and joy. Whether it was the simple joys of everyday life or the act of a family gathering around the bed at night to pray together- I felt unworthy of such things. A lie that I believed for way too long.

This story is not just a recounting of events; it explores scars and stars of finding worth in the rubble of broken dreams. It's about enduring trauma, seizing opportunities, and the arduous journey toward healing and redemption. Beneath the canopy of my past, wrapped in the complexities of life's trials and triumphs, this story unfolds—a narrative etched with the hope of finding light, even in the darkest forests of our lives.

Chapter 1

Roots of Resilience

Growing up in a Christian home, faith was the cornerstone of our family. I didn't know anything other than that life, so I just assumed all kids lived that way. I was proudly raised Pentecostal, which meant never missing a church service, a fellowship meal, revival, a youth event or Vacation Bible School. We had loud, lengthly services and we were there multiple times a week. No service was ever the same and even from a young age, I recognized adults among me that were so in love with the Lord and would fall to their knees to worship Him at every service. Despite our strong faith, I quickly learned that being a Christian didn't mean a trouble-free life. The prayers and church may have been constants, but I began to understand that challenges were all part of the journey.

I often wondered why life seemed more challenging for us than my friends. They seemed to have it all—both parents, fun vacations, and a peaceful home life. I wished for their routine; a sense of predictability was missing in our lives. I'd ponder at night quite often, trying to reconcile my faith with life's uneven distribution of struggles.

I have no memories of my parents together. They split when I was young, so I never got to experience a united family under one roof. The divorce left a gap where a typical family should have been, and I often compared my own to others. I'd envy families who seemed effortlessly close, wondering how life would've been if my parents had stayed together. We moved a lot, never settling for long. My mom worked hard to provide for my older sister and me, so life was always on the go, even as a kid.

My mom remarried when I was young and fortunately for us, he was pretty amazing. He had a kind and gentle soul, loved her deeply and treated us like his own. I was starting kindergarten, loved playing store and was a bit obsessed with Sesame Street. My stepdad's family had a farm, and when we went there, it was like a whole new world to me. I'd always lived near town, minutes from everything, so this was almost like a vacation. I saw new things, smelled new smells, heard new sounds, and made memories I'll always treasure. Like the time their pet turkey (who knew you could have one?) chased me around the pond. I screamed as I ran, leaping into my stepdad's arms and burying my face into his neck with a squeal. I felt safe with him and it's a moment I've never forgotten. Another memory? Stepping in fresh dog poop in the morning as I stepped into the backyard- barefoot. Yeah, it's not the best memory, but it was all part of the adventure for me. It was so different from home; I felt very hopeful there, almost like I was living in a movie.

We lived in a trailer park right outside of town and had a Cocker Spaniel named Lady (I cannot even say this dog's name without a very vivid memory of her wearing my panties when she was in heat). I remember evenings in the sun, loading up our patio table with fruit from the farm, playing cashier and pretending Momma was my customer. It was a new normal I loved, and I remember being genuinely happy there.

Unfortunately, it didn't last long. We abruptly packed up and left one night while my stepdad was at work. I don't remember seeing him again until I was an adult, and I truly struggled for years to make sense of that time. I really loved this man and he was so good to us. I never saw it coming, so I remember feeling sad and confused for quite some time.

Much of that chapter remains hazy amidst the flurry of decisions and the passage of time. Despite the blur, I cherished fond memories from that era, holding onto them to navigate the changes that would soon follow.

My biological father was still very much in the picture at this time as well. The truth is, he was always around during my early childhood. We'd hang out on weekends, and yeah, I was a daddy's girl even though I cared for my stepdad, too, during the time he was with us. When I was with my father, it was all about fun, jokes, pizza, and movies. After my parents split, he married one of my mom's close friends. While I liked her, she never really felt like a mom to me, so I struggled with understanding the dynamic of it all and was ultimately confused about how they ended up together. I loved our visits with him, but often, when we time spent together, it became clear she didn't have any genuine interest in being anything other than a friend to me and my sister. As time passed, their family began to grow, bringing many more changes for us all. I adored my younger siblings, being a big sister was awesome, a change from always being the baby of the family.

Even so, it was tough to see my father starting a new life with someone, struggling to understand why it couldn't have been with Mom. Watching him bond with children who also shared his blood and moments I never had was also hard. I often wondered about their daily routines and family dinners when I left their house. During weekends with them, I felt like an outsider at times. Despite no ill intentions, I never felt I was welcome outside of my weekend visits. This constant sense of being left out fueled some resentment and pain in me, which I only realized much later in life.

The next big wave of change came kind of abruptly, almost like a storm you can sense is coming and suddenly the sky opens up. My mom, always a symbol of strength, had made a cozy nest for us in an apartment complex buzzing with the sounds and sights of a close-knit community and lots of kids. Despite the tight quarters — where we moved in sync as an all-female family — there was a unique charm to it. Our little place was filled with laughter and the clatter of spoons on cereal bowls in the mornings and sometimes even for supper. My sister was in charge of getting me off to school, as well as putting me to bed most nights, so she took on the role of guardian and schoolwork juggler. She was only five years older than me, but she carried herself with quiet strength. Hiding her youth while handling our daily lives with wisdom beyond her years while Mom worked multiple jobs or was out with friends.

I was content with our little life. So when my mom announced she had met someone, a single dad with kids of his own, I remember feeling unsettled and unsure. I vividly remember the moment they arrived to meet me and my sister— sitting on the bottom step of the apartment complex, I was anxiously waiting. When I saw them turning the corner, I raced upstairs to be ready to greet them. I was incredibly nervous, but I could tell from the smile on my momma's face and her high pitched tone that she was excited and somewhat hopeful.

That evening, around a dinner table customarily set for three, the presence of six became a living, breathing symbol of uncomfortable unity and undefined future narratives. As we chewed through a familiar spaghetti dinner and shared hesitant smiles, I felt an unspoken promise and a twinge of uncertainty weave into the fibers of my being, the two emotions intertwined like dissonant threads in a complex tapestry. It was undeniable—the air was dense with the gravity of impending change, and though I sat there surrounded by the sound of unfamiliar laughter, a singular thought resonated clearly in my young mind: Life as I knew it would never be the same again.

They were married just a few months later at my nanny's home, a simple yet promising ceremony. It marked a fresh start for us all, and honestly, each of our families were happy. Shortly after, we then moved into a worn-out house that creaked under the weight of us all. Despite its apparent age, we began to make it a home. The house offered little space and comfort, posing as one of our roughest living situations at that point. With determination and maybe a little imagination, we all embarked on a journey to revamp it. Gradual repairs and renovations took place, with our family's persistence turning the shabby into something dignified. We tackled the cold by insulating windows with plastic and dividing rooms with sheets to keep the warmth in. We even had a kitchen face-off with a rat the size of a small dog once as we began to repair areas of the kitchen. Through all the hardships, we pieced together our sanctuary, shaping it daily into a home that was transformed from the inside out.

With my step-siblings coming and going as they split time with their mother, the whole gang wasn't always around, but life settled into a rhythm. We started school, made friends on our street, and found a little country church nearby. The simple pleasures of rural life filled our days - summers were all about catching crawdads, fishing, and river splashing, while winter turned our surroundings into a snowy wonderland, perfect for sleigh rides on the hills. Christmases were exciting and joyful, with four kids unwrapping gifts and a bunch of family members. It was a taste of the stability every kid wishes for - regular meals, a safe home, warm clothes, and holidays brimming with happiness. For a few memorable years, that sense of normalcy I craved seemed to surround us like a cozy blanket.

From an external perspective, many would perceive it as a tale of redemption. A stepfather enters the scene, rescuing a trio of females, providing stability and protection. That was the story unfolding for quite some time. I remember hearing mumbles among adults we knew, "I'm so glad he stepped in to support them."

Some might recall my childhood as sunny, with my laughter filling our cozy home beside the creek. Yet, my memories paint a different picture — one shadowed by trauma and the struggle to hide a troubled home life. The fear of revealing someone's true nature while coming to terms with the fact that my new stepdad, who had swooped in to save the day, was not who he claimed to be. The pain etching daily into my soul, as I held onto a secret that could literally break everything apart.

The air in rural Virginia was infused with the sweet scent of fresh creek water and the cloying odor of decay, a fitting dichotomy for what lay within the walls of our family home. My story is not one of pity but rather of how pain when grace touches it, becomes a tapestry of resilience and unyielding hope.

ENOUGH ~ 7

Misty "Hope"
Kindergarten, 1991

Chapter 2

Foundations of Fracture

There isn't a specific moment or time frame where I can pinpoint everything shifting, but early memories hint towards subtle changes that happened over time. A few years into my mom's new marriage, as I neared the age of ten, my relationship with my biological father started to show some strain. Our visits became infrequent; plans were canceled at the last minute, and when I did see him, I was met with a layer of uncomfortable ease at times that I couldn't quite put my finger on. One particularly scarring memory was when I accidentally caught my little sister's fingers in the door jam of the hall bathroom, igniting a fury in my stepmother, who scolded me vehemently. Though an accident, the event was painted as an act of jealousy and carelessness, as if to suggest a malicious intent.

As little incidents stacked up, it became apparent that my dad's house dynamics were changing. The result of that meant that I was spending more time at home with my mom and stepdad, who had begun to subtly manipulate my emotions about why my dad didn't want me to come over as much anymore.

I often thought about my father's house - what movies they might be renting from the video store on Friday nights or what type of pizza they ordered, wondering if my favorite was still on the menu.

The transition was gradual, a drip of instability setting the tone for what would eventually become normal. Yet, a defining moment drew a stark contrast between my natural father's affection and my stepdad's mind games as I looked back. One Saturday, my father failed to show up for a planned visit, leaving me waiting anxiously on a stool by the front door, duffle bag at my feet. My stepdad seized this opportunity to taunt me, planting seeds of doubt about my father's love and intentions.

Despite my usual stubbornness and tendency to back-talk, I remained silent that day, swallowing the hurtful words, tears welling in my eyes. Until then, I had never questioned my father's love for me. I had found resolution in believing he was just busy with a job and his other kids, and things were more challenging for him. But, under the weight of my stepdad's cruel words, I began to doubt the affection of the man I believed loved me unconditionally. Or if he loved his "real" kids more, the ones he let live with him all the time. That cruel twist of perception tainted the imperfect but precious life I had strived to see as perfect for so long.

My father never showed up that day, and though I remember receiving a phone call later in the evening with an explanation about a sick sibling, the disappointment had etched itself into my heart. Each subsequent visit with him was shadowed by an unshakable undercurrent of doubt regarding his sincerity and love, but mainly his lack of effort and consistency. Observing my stepdad and his behavior, I now struggle to understand how an adult could deliberately inflict such hurt and plant crippling doubts in the mind of a child. With time, the idyllic image of a blended family that I'd held—safe and content—

began to tarnish behind closed doors. The words and actions echoing within those walls painted a reality far from the harmony and warmth I had once fiercely believed in.

The underlying tension within our blended household was palpable as my step-siblings grappled with their own inner turmoil. Their behavioral pendulum swung wildly, influenced by the stark contrast between our structured, faith-based home and their mother's more laissez-faire approach. As they teetered on the cusp of adulthood, the onerous weight of their choices began to strain the already fragile familial fabric. Their interactions were often volatile: fierce verbal exchanges peppered with profanities, followed by physical altercations that left the walls of our home scarred with fist-sized reminders of the discord. The harmony that once coexisted with our imperfections was swiftly eroded, replaced by a cacophony of blame and hostility.

This domestic battleground was far from the cinematic portrayal of a family triumphing over adversity, and instead, the plot of our lives took a darker turn. At first glance, my stepdad's role in this chaos was ambiguous, shrouded by my willingness to attribute the disarray solely to his children. But as the years unfolded into a wearisome pattern of conflict, I began to discern the more significant, more troubling influence at play. His treatment of my step-siblings was casting a wide net, ensnaring my sister and me in the same cycle of animosity and antagonism. What was once a refuge had become a perpetually unsettling environment, dominated by a daily dose of intimidation and strife.

It began with subtle jabs at my father's character, focusing on his decision to marry my mom's best friend and choose to build a life with her instead. Criticisms would seep into conversations, not just directed at us but extending to my uncles—my mother's brothers—whose imperfect paths were used as ammunition to berate our family's worth. My stepdad's brand of discipline once believed to be a normal expectation, revealed itself to be anything but. He wielded stringent rules with an iron fist, punishing us for significant missteps and mundane actions. Groundings were frequent, and the sting of a belt became an all too familiar sensation. Depending on his level of anger, he'd encourage me to wear more than one pair of pants. We endured tirades about our appearances, decisions, and behaviors, where even how we removed our shoes could lead to drastic consequences. Punishments were meted out for what seemed trifling—like when my sister left milk in her cereal bowl, and she was punished, deeming her selfish and ungrateful. I remember missing meals as a lesson for not finishing the previous night's dinner to his exacting standards. The home became a place of meticulous order, where a misplaced item resulted in revoked privileges and accusations of disrespect. Our once safe space had transformed into a theater of control and punitive discipline.

 I would watch this man raise his hands in church and stand at the altar, proclaiming to be a Godly father who loved children he didn't have to, and I would fearfully dread getting in the car to go home. The confusion was palpable—how could someone flip their personalities at the drop of a hat, leaving us never knowing who we'd get each day? My mom, I think, did the best she could for a long time. She worked a lot, but she was home every evening, and at times, she stepped in to ease situations or smooth over punishments. However, he was the man of the house, and I could tell even her strong-willed spirit and independence were wilting under his thumb. They argued frequently, but he made it clear we'd be on the street without him, and I knew she often swallowed her words to keep a roof over our heads and ensure food was on our table.

 We did leave one night after a very heated, physical argument. I don't remember what it was about, but Mom told us to grab some clothes, and we headed to a nearby motel. My sister ran into the grocery store across the street in her pajamas to get us Pop-Tarts to eat. Ironically enough, the next day was picture day at school, and I had not planned my quick grasp of clothes well. Knowing how our night went and the impulsive choice of clothes, that school picture has always triggered an overwhelming sense of pain. It marks significant moment in my childhood: an abrupt departure, a wrong choice of clothing and hairstyle I'd rather forget, captured in a school picture that would live in an annual yearbook forever. Even today, looking at it hurts my stomach, and I feel that sense of sadness and uncertainty as I smile big for the photographers.

Unfortunately, we quickly returned home. When you don't have anywhere to go, you sadly end up going back. With time, as we were all getting older, I found myself at home a lot with just my stepdad. His kids spent more time at their mom's house for weeks at a time, and my sister started a job. My mom was still picking up some side cleaning jobs here and there. We had a lot of strife between us on a daily basis. He was strict and forceful with words, and his mind games were exhausting. As I got older, my mouth was also persistent in speaking, and I had to get the last word despite the consequences. I did not like the man, and over time, I despised him. For a while, I would tell myself I wouldn't let him have power over me, and he wasn't my real dad, but little did I know what the future seasons of life would bring and how he would overpower me.

I got used to a tough home life, full of arguments, being grounded all the time, and hearing hurtful words like, "You're not good enough for your dad's love, so you're stuck with me. Count yourself lucky. You're fortunate to have me." Holding on to the distant bond with my real father with brief visits here and there, I did whatever it took to make it through each day. I treasured the occasional sleepovers with friends, staying across the street as much as possible, where things felt a bit more normal. I hated being home, though, and I hated that I couldn't tell anyone about it.

I often found solace in daydreams, conjuring up scenarios of freedom and a life unfettered by the chaos of my current one. These mental escapades were respite, a haven I crafted within my thoughts. In the seventh grade, a curious turn of events unfolded when my stepdad decided to enroll me in a private school. Though I hold back from praising the institution entirely, what merits acknowledgment was the close-knit community sentiment that it fostered. Unlike my turbulent home, the school brimmed with laughter, fun memories, weekly field trips, spirited ball games, and an air of normalcy emanating from families I yearned to emulate. Volleyball became my outlet, introducing structure and teamwork, but more poignantly, it led me to my first boyfriend. Then he led me to his family, and they embraced me with an openness I'd never experienced, and I loved being with them. Young or not, I loved this boy and had a genuine friendship with him that I hadn't ever experienced before. We would talk for hours, laugh, and share secrets, and every single time I saw him, I got butterflies. They say you always remember and have affection for your first love, which I believe. What he didn't realize at the time, I'm sure, was the gift he'd given me. The way he smiled at me, held my hand, hugged me, laughed at my jokes, and longed to spend time with me gave me a sense of acceptance and love that I so longed for. I couldn't find that at home and struggled to find in the outside world with friends, but when I found it with him and his family, it was something I wanted to hold onto forever. Being at school, visiting his home, and the many times we were together was a true escape for me, and it felt so good to be someone different when I walked out the door of my home each morning.

As the youngest child now often at home alone, my presence seemed to be oddly comforting to my stepdad at times.

He would leverage these lonely hours to coax me into skipping school when I had a test and needed more time to study, promising the simple joys of a task and then a reward—cutting firewood together and later indulging in ice cream down the road. It's strange how the rarity of good moods and kind gestures can blur the lines of appropriateness and hatred. The first time I played hooky, the guilt was smothered by the thrill of the forbidden and the warmth of fleeting fatherly attention. But as these days became a pattern, a disturbing discomfort began to set in. What initially seemed like benevolent acts would take an unexpected turn, the first time being the evening we returned home for lunch and sat on the sofa to watch television.

    A regular day turned into something unexpected. These instances, disguised as family bonding, started to lead to unwanted behavior invading my personal space and body, which left me confused and unsure. On this day, a line was crossed that I didn't even know needed to be drawn.

    I felt deep down it wasn't right, but the words that accompanied the actions painted a picture of how a father should show love to his daughter. It hit a vulnerable spot in me, making me question everything I knew and felt. Afterward, I got up slowly, walked to my room, and slumped against the door, tears filling my eyes as I softly called out my mom's name. Then I heard the door slam as he left the house like nothing had happened. Emotions rushed in, leaving me unsure of what to do next. I ran to a known but unfamiliar altar in my neighbor's woods, begging God to take me away. I was lost in that moment, not knowing how to escape or what came next when he came back home. I just knew I didn't want to be here anymore. I didn't understand why God couldn't just reach down, pick me up, and put me somewhere else. I kept replaying it in my mind, trying to grasp reality and figure out my next move. I knew what happened wasn't right, but I also knew who he was and how he twisted stories. I felt silenced, not knowing what it meant or who would believe me over him.

There was one evening I was actually home sick that pushed me over the edge. I don't recall how much time was between when it started and stopped, much of it now is a blank space, but I remember the first time and I remember the last time. I was lying in bed, curled under a blanket, with my bedroom door locked. I heard him come home sometime in the early evening and turn my door handle. I could hear frustration on the other side of the door as he messed with the lock. With anxiety flooding my face and my heart pounding, I slipped out and slid under the bed. Moving clothes I'd neglected to put up and a few stuffed animals, I kept sliding back until I could feel the cold sensation of the wall against my side. The door opened, and as I heard his voice, I closed my eyes and silently repeated my over-prayed desire to be taken away at this moment.

As I saw his feet near the corner of my bedpost, he leaned down and laughed at me. With a firm tone, harsh words, and a yank of my arm, he pulled me from underneath my barricade. He had already changed into his pajama pants, which were an indicator of what was to come and demanded I leave my room. With my head down, I followed slowly and sat on the sofa, opposite of him.

I'm not sure what got into me that day, but I vividly recall feeling a surge of anger and disgust when I glanced over at him. It was just pure revulsion. He casually pulled my legs over to his lap, a familiar move at play, and I freaked out. Something inside me just snapped, and I ended up yelling at him before rushing back to my room. Luckily, he didn't follow. Instead, he got dressed and left the house. Fueled by frustration, fear and anger, I boldly grabbed the phone off the wall and called my mom's workplace. When she picked up, I was a complete mess. I couldn't bring myself to spill everything to her, not a chance. I struggled to find the right words to express just enough, so

I shared what I could about what happened that day. It was not the whole picture, not the entire story, but enough that I hoped would make her come home and make us leave him.

I remember the immense sense of betrayal and confusion that washed over me as I put the phone down. The manipulation he'd happily worked against my head and heart was clear, and yet my voice seemed to disappear when it came to speaking out against it. I wanted to scream, to tell her the truth about what had happened, how long and how horrible, but fear welded my lips shut. It was a battle between the need for self-preservation and the desperate desire to be heard and protected.

Clad in confusion, only a child burdened with adult issues could understand; I resolved to be brave when she got home and to stand up to him. I knew every word and decision I made from here was like navigating through a minefield.

Despite the swell of emotions once she came home, I consciously chose to withhold the details. Acknowledging what I had spoken over the phone, I realized facing her and verbalizing the events was beyond my capabilities. The shame, embarrassment, and fear were overwhelming, not necessarily because of her, but due to a broader apprehension of blame and judgment. The subsequent events unfolded in a whirlwind of manipulation and distortion. He convinced my mom that I would fabricate such a story, expressing profound concern over the falsity of my claims. He suggested that his pajama pants had inadvertently come undone in a moment of pure innocence. His narrative painted a picture of my internal turmoil and unresolved issues with my biological father as the catalyst for such an obscene accusation and desire for attention.

The master con artist. The manipulation, the constant lies, and the tangled web we were caught in felt suffocating. After that, nothing else transpired, so if any good came out of it, that was it. Still, having some of my family, our church, and close friends aware of the situation was pretty embarrassing. As far as I know, only adults were in the loop, but I couldn't stand the thought of everyone assuming I'd fabricate such a story.

The weight of it all was a lot. I was furious that nothing had been done about it and that he'd turned the situation back on me. I can't say I was surprised because I knew this man had more faces than even two. He could turn a charm on, and he could manipulate anything and anyone.

Shortly after, on a Sunday morning, while my biological father was dropping me off at church after our weekend, I asked him to stop before we arrived. As he pulled off to the side of the road, summoning all my courage, I looked him in the eye and spilled that my stepdad had been acting inappropriately towards me and manipulating everything. Revealing more details this time. Through tears and hushed sobs, I begged him to let me stay with him and for the truth to be known. It wasn't innocent, and it wasn't my fault.

The gravity of my plea resonated with him as his face softened and his hand warmly enveloped mine. "I'm sorry," he said, his eyes reflecting sincerity. He promised to confront the issue head-on and wouldn't allow my stepfather to go unchallenged. Clutching my duffle bag, we arrived at the church parking lot, and I quietly exited the car. I went straight to the church bathroom and looked in the mirror, thinking this would change everything. He will save me. He has too.

In the following days, I learned that my ordeal had now become the subject of discrete conversations among all of the adults in my life. My mom, my biological father, my stepdad's family, some of my mom's family, and even some church members. A stifling silence took over my home as I anticipated my father's intervention or our departure, the escape I longed for. Yet the outcome was utterly unexpected. My father soon confronted me, his words heavy with disbelief, questioning my motives for weaving such a narrative. In that wrenching moment, any remaining hope and semblance of a relationship with him were irreparably severed. Even 25+ years later, I've never fully recovered from the moment of knowing the one time I needed him the most, my father turned his back on me.

My stepfather, the master of manipulation, constructed an impenetrable facade of lies so convincingly that even those bearing witness were ensnared by his deception. He was the epitome of self-preservation, wielding his words like a practiced swordsman, each striking with intent to distort and confound reality. As the abuse concluded, the psychological torment only intensified - his cruel remarks and mockery of our faith sowed deep rifts within the sutures of our family as he stopped going to church, and the threads began to unravel even further.

We were surrounded by the remains of a truth I once tried to reveal, now buried under his cleverness. We eventually left, seeking shelter in what I can only call the "cottage from hell." Sadly, it was a short-lived escape because it was swarmed with snakes. No exaggeration. Only a few good memories from there, and you might think it was better than what we had before, and you're right. But growing up, we were used to moving a lot and making the most of very little. The last seven years had been hard and, at times, scary, but as he often reminded us - coming back meant we had a home to live in and financial provisions. He reminded us every chance he got that we couldn't survive without him and would make remarks about our return often. Even after returning, we found ourselves discussing in the background how we would eventually break free from this cycle that never seemed to end.

After our final return, the only abuse that continued was that of his mind games. Many times, leaving myself, my mom, and my sister, I think, wondering what the truth was. It's like, you know, but then you second guess everything. Is this better? Will we ever be able to leave? Is he all we truly have?

If you have never lived with a master manipulator and narcissist, it's hard to understand. Why not just leave? Why not just tell the world about him? Why not just escape and reveal his true character to more than your closest circle? It's all we wanted to do, but when you have nowhere to go and no money to support you, your life literally depends on surviving each day.

For years, I battled to channel the hurt towards my mom for staying so long. I struggled for years with the fear of not being worthy enough to be loved, protected, and believed. As I got older, I became more aware that narcissistic behavior is hard to overcome. It's hard to understand, and it's even harder to recover from. I know as an adult now that my mom was dealing with her own demons and fighting to survive, as well as protect us the best way she knew how. I know that her love for me is unconditional, and if anything, I ache for the life she had to live, knowing she was responsible for two others at the same time. To feel like she had no options. I often remember conversations about who would believe us if we told them who he truly was or how he would turn people against us, which happened often. It's like a train that keeps running you over, and you keep getting back up to try and outrun it, only to be knocked down again. Looking back, I realize more than ever all of the unhealthy behaviors, reactions, conversations, and ways of thinking he instilled in us. And yet, we still had a lifetime ahead of us to fight to overcome them and relearn what it means to be loved and respected in a healthy way.

Returning to his home wasn't ideal, but in full transparency, I voted to go back instead of staying in the cottage from hell. The one snake at the door, turned into another snake in the laundry room. Then once we realized you could hear them slithering on the ceiling from the attic above us, I was done. It eerily sounded like someone pulling duck tape off a popcorn ceiling. Terrifying right? I remember asking if there was anywhere else we could go, and with no other options at play, we packed up and went back.

As I got older, I was reminded a couple of times that I voted to return and I do admit that. It was in a therapy session one evening that I shared this story, the realization that even after everything that had happened I still asked to go back. It was the first time I had really said it out loud, "It was just the 3 of us living in this cottage tucked back in the woods. We were already a bit nervous living there, it was dark back there and some sketchy things had happened. Then, we discovered the snakes and that went from finding just 2, to a pure infestation in the attic. The cottage had been empty prior to us moving in and we learned there was legit a land of snakes in the attic. So, when my mom posed the question of where do we go and the only place to go was back, I voted to go back. As a kid, I voted to go the only place she offered for us to go. Either stay with the snakes or return."

I finished saying this out loud and sat in silence. I could feel my therapist's eyes on me and I could sense a rush of emotions overcome me as I realized something profound. I'd carried guilt for that decision for so long, because I felt like my family held me responsible for returning and even worse, wondered if my accusations were even true if I was so willing to return. But, I was a kid. Making that decision shouldn't have been mine. I shouldn't have even been asked after everything that had happened. I was posed with an either or, one of which was horrifying and the other of which we'd done time and time again. Return.

So we did. Amid this fracturing home, the silence among us was so loud. No one was happy, unless you count his ego for knowing we had to come back to have a roof over our head. What none of us realized was the unforeseen and devastating event that loomed on the horizon, irrevocably transforming us all.

Chapter 3

A Profound Sense of Loss

    The warmth and resilience of my nanny's spirit acted as a beacon during the darker epochs at home. Her very presence stitched together the fragments of my childhood with threads of hope and unyielding love; such was the magic of her existence. There was an art to how she blended grace and humility with a relentless devotion to service and God. In her eyes, every challenge was an invitation to lean deeper into faith, propelling her to live a life saturated with compassion and vibrancy. Amidst the disarray that followed her passing, I'm certain she was aware of the turmoil within my heart. She always made herself available to me, listening intently to my trials with parental figures, offering solace without judgment. Her lack of affection for my stepdad was a silent understanding between us, yet her capacity to love remained immense. My most cherished memories are those simple moments we shared—baking sugar cookies, engaging in playful card games, or simply rocking in the gentle ebb and flow of the porch swing with a Fresca in hand. Despite her own strenuous journey through life's trials, her faith and trust in the Lord's path never wavered, and she embraced every day with a conviction that shone brightly, guiding all of us.

She was charismatic, full of joy and, if I'm honest... a little dense at times. I can still hear her voice, her laughter, and that smile that would light up a room. I have memories that could fill pages for weeks. Some that still resonate so profoundly, that I can't help but smile and laugh out loud at. Some of my favorites are my mornings with her after my mom would drop me off, early in the wee hours of the morning, wrapped in a blanket and my pajamas. Having breakfast, taking walks, playing games—it was the best. I'll never forget her putting an egg in the microwave and taking a quick trip next door to check on my great aunt, only to return later with a blown-open microwave door and eggs splattered all over the ceiling. Or that time she called into a radio station on the morning of my birthday and asked them to play my favorite gospel song, and she grabbed my hand and danced around the kitchen with me as we sang "Walk Around My Bedside, Lord."

The simplicity of her approach, her love, her genuine interest in me made me feel like I was on top of the world. To be loved by Betty Ann was a true gift. And to give you just a glimpse into her personality, my family still chuckles at the time she lost her home phone and called her neighbor to come help look for it. The two of them scoured the house trying to find the phone she'd just made a call from. Her little white tennis shoes, her ironed culottes, and those beautiful blue eyes are etched into my soul while the ring of her laughter echoes in my mind.

Losing her just before I became a teenager was life-shattering. My sweet nanny—her absence was an abyss that seemed to devour the light from our family's core. My mom's constant foundation was shattered; my uncle's lives were unhinged. My sister, my cousins, and I—none of us were prepared for the shift in our reality. She had battled a courageous but debilitating fight against cancer, and even in her final days, when she spoke of being ready to "dance on the streets of gold," it did little to fill the chasm inside of me that she once filled. The what-ifs tormented me: could she have been the refuge to whisk me away from my turbulent home life, or would the situation have broken her as well? And amidst the silence left in her wake, I found myself questioning if the God we were raised to serve and follow even understood the depth of how much I needed her.

It's incredibly comforting to believe that a life dedicated to serving God is met with a heavenly embrace when it comes to an end. Even though it leaves a deep void, the thought of being reunited in the afterlife can be both bitter and sweet for believers. Our family, despite going through life's storms had stayed connected through traditions rooted in love and shared faith. My mom's side of the family was full of love, life and intentional relationships. From holiday gatherings and Sunday dinners, to Easter celebrations and cousin sleepovers, these moments were a testament to a bond that I think we assumed even death could not break.

At 37, memories of my nanny and her warm embrace still linger, like a distant melody that bridges the gap of years. I can almost smell the faint scent of her lotion and feel the softness of her hug. Her loss shook us to the core. Eventually our family's fabric started to unravel, and the cherished traditions of my youth slowly faded away, leaving behind a lingering sense of disappointment that I thought she would share. Her passing brought forth a season of grief and silence, a prelude to a story that would forever shape our family. I share this next chapter of our family not expecting empathy, as it's a path that's hard to understand unless you've walked in its shadow. It's simply a raw and transformative tale, marked by loss and the ever-elusive hope for redemption.

Just a couple of years after my nanny's passing, our family would face yet another tragedy. Another deep loss. A young girl, known to our family, vanished without a trace, sending shockwaves of distress throughout our small town. The thick veil of anxiety and dread was only worsened when, a grueling few weeks later, her lifeless body was discovered. It was a harrowing incident that seemed to stop time itself, but what followed would cut even deeper into our already wounded family's heart. My uncle, a familiar face at every family gathering, a man intertwined with many of my childhood memories, was arrested and charged with the young girl's murder.

Navigating through the complexities of grief and disbelief, I find myself grappling for words to reflect upon this nightmarish episode of my life. It remains a painful sliver of reality to confront, even as time marches on. I won't feign detachment or imply that the anguish of reliving these events has diminished. Indeed, being indirectly linked to such a heinous crime exposes a harsh truth: you are often judged by another's sins, scrutinized beneath the unforgiving lens of the public. The media's invasive eye and the community's swift judgment became our new, unwelcome companions. Yet, in the shadows of such a brutal and public calamity, you learn a difficult lesson about human connections, discovering a circle of genuine support - those who stay by your side and those who don't - even when your connection to the incident is but a shared surname. I can actually still feel the sting of looks and whispers as we walked into church, school or local gatherings. That is a kind of pain that is hard to overcome.

The moment I found out is unfortunately a core memory I recall clearly. I remember my mom coming into my room one evening before bed, sitting softly beside me as she pulled me in close to her. Her eyes swollen and red from tears, I swallowed knowing whatever was going to come out of her mouth was not good news. She told me that my uncle had been arrested for the murder and the following morning as I sat at my friends house waiting for our traditional ride to school, I would encounter the first harsh reality of seeing my uncles face plastered on the morning news. That day, that moment, is forever etched into my soul and I can still feel the fear, frustration and confusion that was suffocating every breath I tried to take.

What followed this event was what you'd imagine—a trial, grueling and painful, unearthing family secrets no one wished to acknowledge. Days filled with questions leading nowhere, testimonies that seemed to only deepen the pain, and the heavy truth that no amount of scrutiny would make sense of the senseless. Closure remained elusive; questions lingered without answers, leaving only the raw reality of loss and mourning for two families—one, of course, bearing an incalculable weight.

I rarely speak of this chapter to anyone, but honesty compels me to acknowledge its weighty impact, not only on me, but on our entire family. My uncle, a central figure in my life who affectionately gave me my nickname, "Hopey," never missed a moment that mattered. He was there, always—a pillar, a father figure from my youngest days. Despite his grave missteps, he is and always will be family. His life sentence behind bars, devoid of hope for release, is a shadow we live with daily, a source of persistent frustration and heartache.

This narrative, as painful as it is, is not told for mere catharsis. Rather, it's shared in the face of loss—my nanny's, whose heart would have broken even more had she witnessed these subsequent trials. Then there was my mom, grappling with her mothers absence and facing a trial no one can truly be ready for, losing her brother and all of this amidst the anticipated dissolution of her turbulent marriage. Sometimes, I am left to ponder the depths of resilience a person holds within.

Any hope of our family reuniting, of mending the broken gaps, became hopeless. There is no way to make sense of a tragedy like this, and no matter how much time has passed, everyone's feelings remain raw and unhinged. The room is left thick with resentment, pain, confusion, and profound loss. The ties that once bound us together have frayed, seemingly beyond repair for some, as we each grapple with the reality of what has occurred and the stark finality it has imposed on us. The shared surname, once a symbol of unity, now marks the chapters of our shared affliction.

As a family, we have faced a lifetime of pain, uncertainty and unknowns. A roller coaster of tremendous pain, tragedy, and abuse with a glimmer of hope now and then. Looking back as an adult, I see this was a breaking point for my mom. The trial nearly destroyed her, and I know we lost parts of her in that chapter that we'll never recover. My heart aches for all she went through as she tried to come to terms with losing her baby brother due to such a heinous decision, all while trying to be a mother and shield us from the public. As a mom now, I understand the fierce protectiveness I feel for my kids, recognizing the choices I have that she didn't. The profound losses we endured back to back, led to our family slowly unraveling over time.

My moms side of the family, once incredibly close grew distant over time. For me, this was another significant loss as I was incredibly close to my aunts, uncles and cousins. Death changes you. A tragedy changes you. It seemed to happen in slow motion as the family began to dismantle. While we may not talk often, you can be assured with a phone call they would still show up. When we are together, which is very seldom, we are quickly reminded of the laughter and love that once bonded us. While the wounds of our past may never fully heal, we have found solace in creating new memories within our own families and cherishing the moments from way back when. It's still painful to me as an adult to see the distance between us. I'm thankful for social media and having the ability to see their lives continue, even though I mourn the loss often of what we could have had.

One thing I've realized is that tragedy can either bring people together or cause separation. Honestly, I think it happened without intent because everyone was just trying to survive and move on. The voyage through loss is indeed a life-altering journey, and its power to paralyze is formidable. The most profound grief is perhaps in the loss of someone still living, a presence absent not by death but by the chasm of the inexplicable. All my life, I've trodden carefully through life's numerous chapters, addressing each one with a deliberate gentleness. This season of loss, a chapter long deferred, now confronts me with its stark and unyielding reality. My visits to the cemetery are bittersweet—a place where stories are told and tears mix with laughter as I recount my adulthood to a silent stone and the ethereal comfort of my nanny's spirit. Yet, the harrowing task of visiting a prison looms—a visit rife with emotional turbulence, an ordeal we barely whisper about, as if the silence might keep the sad history at bay.

I live with this dread and unwelcome intrigue of online sleuths that one day may stir up long-settled dust, therefore my path towards healing demanded confrontation with unaddressed scars. It required more than therapy; it demanded direct engagement with the painful past. And so, in the sovereignty of my mid-thirties, I armed myself with court documents, embarking on a meticulous journey through every page, statement, and transcript from the trial. For weeks I sat in my office floor surrounded by thousands of documents and boxes, making a timeline of events while trying to connect memories. In seeking resolution, I found no grand epiphany that explained the crime. However, clarity pierced through the haze of my memories, illuminating the uncertainties that shadowed my understanding of people and events from that time. It was not the content of the documents but the act of facing them that endowed me with a newfound strength to put this chapter behind me—one that embodies the essence of resilience and provides a foundation upon which I continue to build my future.

Even as the chapters of adversity filled the book of my life, I came to realize that every experience, however dark, shaped the foundation of my existence. I became adept at compartmentalizing, boxing away each calamity with the hope of moving forward unburdened by their oppressive weight. As a teenager seeking love's embrace, my yearning led me down a labyrinth of senseless choices. I pushed away solace, defensively bracing for betrayal and abandonment, a pattern too familiar in my life's tapestry. Trust was a luxury I couldn't afford, a fragile gift always on the brink of shattering. Feeling a lack of worthiness and acceptance, I found myself driven by these emotions in many of my decisions and relationships. The desire to be valued became a significant influence in shaping my life. Oftentimes leading to poor decisions, trusting others I shouldn't and looking for value, worth and love in all the wrong places.

My journey illustrates the profound impact that life's tribulations can have on the soul. I've learned that neglect, trauma, betrayal, and loss can fashion a prison of the mind, just as potent as any cell of iron and concrete. Yet clinging to unprocessed pain is like clutching a barbed wire—it only deepens the wounds. Ignoring my history was merely a temporary reprieve, a false promise that denied the strength and growth that come from facing one's deepest fears and pains.

Through faith, I've come to understand that we are not simply given what we can handle, but rather, life unfolds in unpredictable chapters, often shaped by human fallibility and marred by sin. Yet in these pages of misfortune, we have a choice—we can succumb to the echoes of our past, or rise with resilience, reconstructing from the rubble a testament to our enduring spirit.

My Momma & Nanny

Chapter 4

The Fragile Quest to Belong

Resilience is the ability to adapt and bounce back from adversity, trauma, or stress. It is not a trait you are born with, potentially influenced by genetic factors yes, but instead it's a skill that can be developed and strengthened over time. Like building a solid foundation for a house, building resilience requires effort and determination. It involves actively facing and processing difficult experiences rather than avoiding them.

In my journey towards healing, I learned that resilience is not about being strong all the time or never experiencing pain. It is about recognizing that despite our struggles and suffering, we have the capacity to heal and grow. It is about acknowledging our vulnerabilities and using them as sources of strength rather than weaknesses. For me, this meant facing my past traumas and repressed emotions head-on. It was not easy, and at times, it felt like I was reliving the pain all over again. But as I worked through my past with the help of therapy, lots of prayer and support from loved ones, I began to understand the underlying causes of my struggles and learned healthier ways to cope and move forward.

Healing is not a linear process. There will be ups and downs, good days and bad days. But as I continued to make progress, I realized that the sound of healing is often silent. Sometimes, it's a quiet whisper telling us to keep going, reminding us of our inner strength and resilience. It's the small moments of peace and happiness that we can find amidst the chaos and pain.

I also learned that healing is not a destination but rather an ongoing journey. It is a continuous process of self-discovery and growth. Along the way, I have found comfort in connecting with others who have gone through similar experiences; through the act of storytelling, people connect. We can learn from each other and support one another on our paths towards healing.

Furthermore, I have come to realize the significance of self-care, self-compassion, and the decisive act of forgiveness. It was not until I hit rock bottom, sinking into a depression, that I used to belittle when others couldn't simply "snap out of it" that I truly understood the depth of my pain. I despise the term "daddy issues," but I must acknowledge its reality. It represents a realm of anguish that I wouldn't wish upon anyone.

After my uncle's trial concluded, we left my stepdad and relocated to a new town when I was nearly 14. One evening, my mom took my sister and me for a drive and shared that her various side jobs had financed this fresh start. She had dedicated numerous late nights to cleaning and preparing the new place for us. The property's owners, a compassionate and established couple in the community, graciously offered us safety and welcomed us with open arms. Understanding my mom's financial hardships and our urgent need to move, they struck a deal with her: she would clean and prepare the property in exchange for forfeiting the deposit. This new home was unlike anything I had ever known. A tiny mobile home, nestled on vast land, it overlooked a serene pond at the rear of the couple's property. When looking up the definition serenity, in my book anyway, there is a picture of this place next to it.

It marked a fresh beginning that inevitably set us on a new path. As time went by, my sister got married and moved out, my mom immersed herself in work, and I transitioned to homeschooling, leaving me alone at home a lot. Amidst the anticipation of new possibilities, it was also a transition period for me. At 14, I had already faced significant challenges, and only in later years did I realize that this phase of my life would profoundly influence the person I am today and the future that awaited me. In this vulnerable stage, escaping an unspoken past and adjusting to a life filled with change, I yearned for acceptance, love, and a sense of worth beyond my mother. So when a 19-year-old boy turned his head towards me and caught my eye, there wasn't an alarm loud enough or a bright red flag sufficient to signal me to turn away.

I was a child. I know this. I also understand that most of you are likely saying, "I'd never let my daughter." And you know what, I get that. As a mother myself now, I'm quite certain I'd have the same response.

Admittedly, I didn't look or act like a typical 14-year-old. Initially, he had clarified that he assumed I was older, around 16 or 17. Despite this, the situation progressed to multiple dates, all of which my mom was present for. Over time, a friendship developed, leading to a close connection with a young man who made me feel secure. Despite facing gossip and scrutiny, we eventually transitioned into a genuine relationship after enduring almost a year of my mom being the third wheel wherever we went and whatever we did.

I felt a real sense of purpose and love with this guy. He looked at me like I was the only one in the room, and I truly felt loved. We had deep conversations and shared a significant bond through childhood experiences, and I trusted him completely. It may have seemed odd, but as my family and friends got to know him, it became clear that age didn't matter, and we were happy together. At times, without a word, he would notice my thoughts wandering to painful memories, gently lifting me in his arms to divert my attention. His hands would cradle my face frequently, affirming me with positive words, leading to conversations about a shared future. I felt like I'd hit a gold mine, like everything I'd endured had led me to this moment and this person.

I did sometimes grapple with the age gap between us, as he was 19 and immersed in a world I had yet to explore. Despite my reservations, the thought of losing him was unbearable. I devoted my heart and soul to him, hoping he could mend my brokenness. While not the wisest choice for a vulnerable teenage girl, the comfort and affection he provided felt like a lifeline. I entrusted him with my broken heart and damaged body, and I genuinely thought that he had repaired them. I experienced pure joy. I recall a Sunday evening drive with the windows down, the sun casting its warm glow, and we crooned to an old country melody. I stole a glance and caught a smirk on his face. His hand reached for mine, affirming my belief that this was it. This was the life I yearned for, the life I truly deserved after all I had endured.

Approaching our two-year milestone in the relationship coincided with his 21st birthday, shedding light on our significant age difference once again and introducing new obstacles. His late nights gradually turned into all-nighters, weekends filled with new friends and nightclubs while I remained home. A familiar sense of longing grew more robust, casting doubts on the path ahead, and I found myself questioning everything I had believed in us. The trust was broken, lies came to light, and my heart, over time, began to shatter. Shards of the same pieces he'd spent 2 years carefully putting back in place were now coming undone by his very hands. Our families had forged strong connections, we had shared meaningful milestones, and

I sincerely believed he was my forever love. He was the first person I had fully entrusted with my broken heart, shared my childhood pain with, and felt understood without having to explain myself. What would my life be like without him? At 16, such thoughts seemed like the end of the world to me.

While I was crafting my own fairy tale and sometimes trying to keep it together, my mom was navigating her own story. She had sworn off relationships, so the idea of her starting anew didn't cross my mind. Unexpectedly, a friend introduced her to someone whose life quickly intertwined with ours. It felt so natural as if it were supposed to happen. He entered our world with genuine love that we could feel from all angles. My sister and I were captivated by his caring nature and charismatic demeanor. Knowing he had kids of his own, we felt a sense of fatherly comfort from him and he handled our situation and trauma with incredible sensitivity. When he decided to marry my mom, he sought our approval, revealing volumes about his character. The prospect overjoyed us, and I was excited to embark on a new journey, witnessing my mom's joy and genuine love. Her newfound confidence, genuine smile, and laughter warmed my heart. It marked a significant season of change, one that I embraced. By the time they got married, I had broken up with my boyfriend and threw myself into the adventures of being a teenager, driving, a new home, a new life, new friends, and a new job.

In general, I wouldn't label myself as a bad kid. Admittedly, I've made some unwise choices and been in multiple relationships - some I regret, a few I cherish. On reflection, I recognize that I sought love and approval in the wrong places, yearning for a sense of value and significance. I mostly turned to boys for this, as I had few close female friends. I seemed to have a talent for befriending those I couldn't trust not to talk about me behind my back after they hugged my neck, so I kept my inner circle small. While juggling a full-time job and striving to complete my education, I was determined to always be in a relationship. This perspective on life was far from healthy, leading me to heartbreak, a constant yearning for something more, and many regrets. Sometimes, I wondered if it was just being a teenager or if there was something else I was constantly trying to fill.

One might wonder why that was, considering I finally had everything I'd ever wanted. Our new home was wonderful. I loved where we lived, and I had a true, pure and honest family for the first time in my life. We had a beautiful, safe home filled with countless memories and milestones. From riding horses, raising puppies, family meals, and vacations I'll forever cherish, I had finally found the kind of safety that comes from having two loving parents take care of you, both of whom wanted to be there for you. Despite this gift, I always craved more - seeking acceptance, recognition, value, and someone willing to spend time with me. My first serious relationship was with someone five years my senior, who made grand promises but failed to deliver. That experience matured me, exposing me to things I shouldn't have known at my age and a lifestyle I began to yearn for and struggled to forget. He was the first person I trusted completely, learning things about me that no one else knew, making it hard for me to focus on who I was by myself. Who was Hope? What did she genuinely desire? Who was she without a boyfriend? Could I find fulfillment in healthier pursuits? Why can't I have a bunch of girlfriends to chill with and not worry about the guys? Doubt, pain, and fear of rejection kept popping up everywhere around me.

I never let myself explore this. I just went from one relationship to another during my teens. That pattern stemmed from avoiding the pain inside me, the trauma I had boxed up neatly, tucked away in a corner. Growing up, I often wondered why my mom permitted that relationship. As a parent now, I can't fathom my child, at 14, confiding in me about wanting to date a 19-year-old. I questioned how I would react in such a situation. One Saturday, during my early twenties, we delved into parenting challenges while visiting my mom. Reflecting on what I might face as a girl mom, I gathered the courage to ask her, "Why did you let me date someone so much older than me when I was just a kid?"

Her response honestly didn't surprise me because she probably... unfortunately wasn't wrong. It was not easy to admit, but she was concerned that if she said no, knowing how vulnerable I was, I might rebel and intentionally make a decision that would change our lives for good. At first, I was shocked, but when I look back at who I was, how I felt, and how he made me feel after everything I'd been through... she was probably right. Whether it was right or wrong, I respect her choice to be our third wheel for almost a year. And I am honestly thankful for her decision to allow it to happen. While that relationship brought a lot of pain, I don't regret it. A big part of who I am, who I've become, and how I survived that phase of life comes from that experience. It's a part of my story that connected seasons together and it's an era of learning, love, loss and vulnerability. All of the things I'd need later in life. Was it right? I don't know. However, for the 14-year-old me who was broken and searching for a place to belong, it turned out to be a comforting spot for quite a while, shaping a lot of who I am.

While life was good - like, really good... a new stepdad whom I adored, a new family, and a new home brought many changes. Normal felt so lovely. Pitching in at my stepdad's business, learning to ride horses, and spending time with him on the weekends, I got super close to him. It didn't take long for me to start calling him "Dad," and he very naturally became one of my best friends. I ended up opening up to him more than my mom. The trust I had with him was something I'd never known, and I truly love him with my whole heart. As his daughter, I believe he's capable of anything and knows the answer to any question and solution to any problem and will always be there. As a successful small business owner, he's inspired me to set higher goals, have big dreams, and work hard. He always knows how to make me laugh, even when I'm feeling down, and his words of wisdom guide me through tough times.

Through all the ups and downs of life, my stepdad has been a constant source of love and support. He showed me what it means to be an actual father figure - someone who is there for you no matter what, loves you unconditionally, and always has your back. He has taught me so much about perseverance, dedication, and hard work - qualities I carry daily.

But most importantly, my stepdad showed me what a loving relationship looks like. With him and my mom, I saw how two people can trust, respect, and love each other deeply. I was and will forever be grateful daily for my stepdad's presence. He has taught me so much and continues to inspire me to be the best version of myself. And while he may not have raised me from birth, he will always be my dad in every sense of the word.

He was often the one to try and lessen my punishment after Mom found out about a party I went to or a place I drove I shouldn't have. He was there to joke, make me laugh, and teach me everything I know about cars, horses, business, and true love.

On my 18th birthday, I visited the social services office and legally adopted my stepfather's last name. This decision was deeply personal; I longed for my name to align with his, as I felt a strong bond with him. As I drove towards downtown, my phone rang. It was my biological father, not calling to wish me well on my special day but to inform me that his insurance would no longer cover me due to reaching adulthood. This stark contrast in behavior highlighted the unwavering love and support I received from my stepdad. Standing in the parking lot, a wave of pride washed over me as I readied myself to embrace the title of the man who, in every way, had indeed become my father.

Reflecting on my relationship with him, whom I'm proud to call "dad," I am reminded of his profound impact on shaping who I am today. I believe anyone can be a father; it is just the biological part of creating life. But being a dad, that's a whole different story. It's about choosing, showing love, and always being there. He taught me the true meaning of unconditional love and showed me that family is not just about blood but about the bonds we create through love and support.

He taught me the values of forgiveness, understanding, and patience, which continue to shape my relationships. I found solace in confiding in him, as he sought to understand and support my aspirations and identity. He became my voice of reason, a steadfast companion, and has been by my side through life's greatest moments. From walking me down the aisle to witnessing the birth of my children, he has never missed a milestone for me or them. While we've faced our fair share of challenges, his commitment to keeping our communication open, our relationship strong, and our bond pure fills me with pride to call him MY dad.

Dear Dad,

As I write down my story and reminisce about my past, a flood of words pours onto the paper, overwhelming me with the sentiments I wish to express to you. Therefore, I have chosen to carve out a special place within my book to compose letters to the cherished individuals who have significantly influenced the person I am today.

From the very beginning, you embraced me with open arms, offering me a love so profound and unconditional, that it altered the course of my life in the most beautiful way. You didn't just step into our lives; you brought along a light illuminating a path of healing we desperately needed. For every moment since, for every lesson taught and love given, I am eternally grateful.

You walked me down the aisle, a testament to your unwavering support and the shared bond we've cultivated over the years. Watching you hold my children for the first time, seeing your eyes light up with the same love and kindness you've always shown me, reaffirmed what I've always known—your love knows no bounds.

It's not just in these monumental moments that your influence shines. It's in the everyday guidance, the life skills you passed on with patience and humor—from teaching me how to drive a 5-speed, sharing the exhilarating freedom of spinning donuts, to the careful precision of driving in snow. Your lessons went beyond the technical; you taught me resilience, creativity, and the joy of life's ride.

You inspired me to dream big, work hard and to keep climbing. Watching you, learning from your ethic and passion, gave me the courage to carve my own path. You've shown me that with hard work and determination, dreams can become reality.

But perhaps, the most significant lesson you've imparted is how to love and be loved. Through your actions, you've demonstrated the power of unconditional love, the strength it imbues, and the upliftment it offers. You've made it unequivocally clear—I am worth love, and I am enough. That invaluable gift has been my guiding light, illuminating my own path to self-acceptance and worth.

The surname I proudly bear is a symbol of our bond, a testament to the family we've built together, not by blood, but by choice, by love, by shared life experiences. You calling me your own has been the greatest honor of my life.

*In writing this, I realize words can hardly encapsulate the depth of my gratitude and love for you. Thank you for staying, for choosing to be my dad, my mentor, my confidant, and for showering me with love that has shaped me into the person I am today. Your legacy, one of love, strength, and unwavering support, will forever live on through me. I am proud to be **your** daughter.*

Love you big,

Butterfly

Me & My Daddy
December 2005

Chapter 5

When You Know, You Know

Being homeschooled, as well as moving to a new town means having only a few friends. Through work and finally having my drivers permit, I did began to meet new people. While I'd consider the fact I was friendly with a few, my social circle was nearly non-existent. This was also the era of AIM and Myspace, so most conversations I was having were online and the idea of a fun Friday night in our town meant hanging out at the gas station. There was one local girl I had befriended quickly and she actually switched into my homeschooling program with me. So over time, we became quite close and we evolved into very tight friendship over the years.

One evening, I had stopped by our local drive-in for dinner with my mom when one of the cooks came out to the car— handing me a piece of paper with his phone number on it, asking me to go on a date the following night. Reluctantly, I accepted. This boy was sweet and a true Southern charmer, but it was immediately apparent that this wouldn't go further than friends. I said yes, and little did I know that night would be a memory I'd cherish forever.

We grabbed some food and cruised along some back roads, and he asked if we could swing by to meet his friends. I had been living in this town for a while now, but the field parties and hangout spots in the woods were sometimes out of the norm for me still. Nevertheless, as we parked and I casually crossed a creek bed in my flip-flops, I saw a group of guys chilling by a fire near a small cabin and pond. Walking up the bank, my date introduced me to the first guy we approached, "This is Shortt." With one heck of a smile on his face, this dude comes closer to me and reaches out, looks at me, makes eye contact, and casually goes, "You want a beer?"

If I could have melted, I totally would have. What a pickup line, huh? Apparently it didn't take much for me back then. Mom, don't worry...I said no, but I couldn't stop sneaking glances at him all night, and his smile almost crushed my soul. His smile, vibe, laugh, eyes, and voice made me instantly nervous. Something about him seemed so carefree, and I was drawn to him for reasons I'm still unsure of. Even after we left, it was stuck in my head. I ended up bombarding my date with questions on the way home - I wanted to dig deeper into this guy: his name, age, job, family... you know, the whole shebang. Poor dude probably wished he'd never asked me out that night.

As I strolled away from my date's truck, I rushed up the steps to our home to find my folks all cozy, watching TV together as usual. With a smile on my face and some curious glances, my dad goes, "Date went well?" And I replied, "Eh, it was okay. But I found the guy I'll marry one day." My mom rolled her eyes, dad chuckled, and I ended up sharing the story with them, skipping the beer part.

Yes, this sounds a bit dramatic, but that's how the night played out. My dad knew who he was and knew his family, and the smile on his face told me that it wasn't such a bad idea to pursue. I remember turning to go downstairs to my room and said with a smile, "When you know, you know."

Deep down, as I went to sleep that night, I had a feeling this "Shortt" kid I just met would take me on quite the roller coaster ride.

And boy, was I right.

Shortly after we met, he finally asked me out on our first date, which ended up being at a demolition derby. He didn't kiss me that night, but he held my hand while driving my car and kept glancing at me with a smirk. You know, the kind that makes a girl's heart skip a beat and helps her forget all the heartache she's experienced. Also, it's the kind that makes you throw all reservations out the window.

We eventually made it official, leading to an on-and-off relationship that felt like an endless roller coaster. He struggled with decisions, weighing whether to choose me or not. Honestly, I thought it was just immaturity. Each time I wanted to end it, I couldn't help but think about the times when it was just us, cruising down back roads with Nickelback blaring; it just felt right. Being with him brought such comfort, and those butterflies never went away. I didn't just like this boy, I was crazy about him. It's so hard to explain it, but it was a unique feeling I struggled to understand at times and one I could not ignore. BUT, our relationship was messy and it wasn't easy.

After a year of heartbreak, I decided to walk away. Despite being the same age, I had already weathered a lifetime of challenges and sorrows, which had matured me beyond my years. I couldn't deal with the indecisiveness, which now I realize was him just being a teenage boy.

Following the breakup, a whirlwind of events unfolded swiftly. Little time had passed between departing my childhood home, embarking on a journey of personal growth through my first serious relationship, welcoming a new stepfather, settling into a new residence, obtaining my driver's permit, securing a new job, entering a new romantic relationship, and enduring a profound heartbreak that seemed impossible. Suddenly, I found myself in another phase of vulnerability. I never sat still long enough to process anything, and instead, I just kept running to the next thing. Looking for love, looking for acceptance, and wanting attention seemed to be an uncontrollable void I longed to fill. Toss in a couple more relationships, and just about the time I'd decided I had moved on and was planning a different future for myself, my phone rang.

That "Shortt" kid.

All defenses crumble. A smile I attempt to conceal breaks through.

A quick hello, a sincere apology, and a brief "I love you" were enough to make me drop everything and run back. I loved this boy. I'm sure my parents wanted to smack me, but I dove back in with his promise: This was it.

There was no hesitation in me; I knew this was the boy I had been sure of, and I leaped at the chance to embrace a future with him.

Because when you know....you know.

When I recount this next chapter of our story, I sometimes ponder what I would advise if my daughter returned home declaring she was poised to embark on a similar path. Less than a year after that redemptive phone call, Ryan and I exchanged vows at the tender age of 19. With hesitant parents on each side, we possessed a shared conviction that kept doubt at bay, and we felt little need to justify our choice to anyone. The decision to marry was sudden, spurred perhaps by my fear that the boy might backtrack. But in 2005, amidst a bitter ice storm, I married my high-school sweetheart, my steadfast partner, Ryan. It's elusive, that specific charm he holds, but since that night we first met, he'd captured my heart, and throughout the years, I repeatedly found myself returning in search of it. We were young, brimming with love for each other, and oblivious to future trials; we pledged to navigate them together.

Admittedly, our dating period was brief and perhaps impetuous, but over time, as I divulged the fragments of my troubled past to him, Ryan never once cast judgment or voiced skepticism. Instead, he offered an ear, shoulder, and heart, providing solace whenever shadows of my history loomed large. Unbeknownst to him, no handbook exists on how to love and grow old with a woman whose life is a tapestry woven from threads of abuse, trauma, and uncertainty. Even armed with resolve, tenacity, and a healthy dose of obstinance, there were moments when I grappled with a deep-seated sense of unworthiness and the daily task of accepting myself truly and wholly.

Ryan's understanding surpassed mere companionship; he became a vigilant guardian of my healing. It was so much more than feeling safe with him. I felt understood, I felt accepted. I felt like he was gently holding broken pieces of myself and carefully handling them in hopes that we'd put them back in place together. He learned the intricacies of my past, the truths that haunted my dreams, ensuring to approach with tenderness rather than surprise. Unbeknownst to him, his love and ability to truly see me sparked incremental healing within my very bones. Although I carried the weight of unresolved emotions, I found solace in our conversations, decisions, and the chapters of our life together. I often sat alone in my car after running errands or finishing work, reflecting on the journey that led me here. "This is my life," I would think, "I have survived, overcome, and discovered a love that is reciprocated. I have a future, a family. While some parts may be fractured and many wounds remain, we have emerged on the other side."

When tough arguments arose, my instincts often urged me to flee, a habitual response rooted in a lifetime of instability. Yet, Ryan stood firm with resolve, his eyes earnest; he'd remind me, "No, you're going to take a moment, and then we can talk it out. But tomorrow, we'll wake up and try this again." His tenacity was a testament to his commitment, teaching me that love isn't a battlefield for abandonment but a sanctuary where patience and persistence converge to overcome even the deepest-seated fears.

Often, I would question whether I truly deserve the acceptance and love that surrounds me. He comes from an extraordinary family, one that I felt unworthy of. Our lives intertwining gave me two sets of grandparents, aunts and uncles, and even a sibling. I was in awe of their closeness, how every celebration included everyone, and how they all lived on the same farm, stretching miles down one road. A significant part of why I loved him so profoundly and yearned for a life with him was the knowledge that I would become a part of that loving family.

He really balanced me out. He's always been the carefree type, you know? Growing up surrounded by noise, there's this peaceful silence that just settles in when he's around. Back when we were younger and just starting out, being with him made me see myself differently and gave me a sense of hope for the future he proved to me I did deserve. And that smile never failed to light up my day and fill my heart with joy. I was crazy about this guy, and I tried not to take it for granted that he was, in fact, now my husband.

Ryan worked hard to provide for us, and we both busted our butts to pay what little bills we had and navigating life together. Pioneers among our peers, we were married before our friends embarked on such a journey; without footsteps to follow, we learned to stride in our own rhythm. Our modest abode was a cute little mobile home, its interiors lovingly adorned in a questionable tapestry of country Americana decor, and despite its size, it was a castle built upon the pride of our achievements. Then, about ten months into our marriage, the unexpected happened.

I was on my way to work one morning, when a brief moment of nausea suddenly forced me to pull over and I found myself throwing up on the side of the road. I called my sister that morning in a panic, knowing that a random moment of throwing up in the morning was a solid sign of one thing and one thing only. She calmed my nerves enough for me to get through the first half of the day and I purchased a pregnancy test on my lunch break. Once back at work, I escaped to the restroom, my heart pounding as I waited for the result. The lines on the test appeared quickly, undeniably positive. In the solitude of that tiny bathroom, I met my gaze in the mirror of the doctor's office where I worked. Tears threatened to spill as a heavy weight settled in my chest. For a brief, crushing moment, I was consumed with doubt. "I am not fit to be a mother. I am not worthy of being responsible for someone else's life when mine as a child was such a mess," I thought, the enormity of the journey ahead daunting. I had doubts about my ability to raise a child within a family unit, providing them with protection, nurturing, and shielding them from a life resembling my own.

I'm unsure if our parents were thrilled, terrified or a little bit of both when we announced our pregnancy a few months later. My sister was super excited and started sharing clothing and baby advice with me, just like Ryan's sister, who asked us to babysit her newborn and gain some experience. By this time in my life, I had lost touch with my biological father and stepmom—a source of inner turmoil due to the years missed with my younger siblings and the moments they were not a part of. The pain wasn't borne from their absence alone but amplified by the void of those connections lost. Yet, any possibility of reconciliation as adults had slipped away after I announced my engagement at 18.

On the day of our wedding shower, my mother pulled me aside, her voice a lance of worries piercing the celebration, to convey that my biological father and stepmom wouldn't be attending. They had reached out to her, voicing their concerns over a rumor they had heard that I was concealing a pregnancy—a stark irony against the reality that no secret could outlast the physical truth of time. While there wasn't much left between us, on the evening of my bridal shower, any threadbare hope of mending familial ties frayed beyond any sort of repair. The crushing realization that I may never suffice for my biological father's endorsement broke through the surface as an adult. His absence that night, compounded by what transpired after, shattered the facade. Their words (his and my stepmoms), tainted with accusation, mirrored her belief I was a wayward teen masking my true intentions for marriage—they cut deep, triggering a rare moment where my mother's patience crumbled. She bravely intervened, severing the cycle of his neglect. Her defense of me signaled the end of an era—she had always painted his image in forgiving strokes, weaving excuses for me to cling to, nurturing a hope within me for an affection that was never forthcoming. She had harbored a desire for us to bridge the growing chasm. Still, with every chance given, my stepmom emerged, disruptive as a storm, with my father fading into her shadow, his passivity silent acquiescence to the chaos she wrought.

So, I'd not only grown up and wed without them in my life, but in March of 2007, we became parents and entered another chapter without them. The birth of our daughter was a wild ride, almost taking my life, but in the end, it resulted in her arriving a bit earlier than expected, bringing us so much joy, as well as a lot of fear. She came into the world five weeks ahead of schedule, a tiny bundle of life, while a big group of friends and family filled the hospital corridor to show their support. The early days of parenthood were a rollercoaster, from dealing with those infamous black tar-like newborn stools to the never-ending, sleepless nights filled with her cries. It tested our resilience in ways we couldn't have imagined. Our daughter, Braylee, was as tiny as a child's toy, and I constantly questioned my maternal instincts, wondering if we could care for someone so delicate. When we were alone at home during the day, I held her out in front of me and wept, promising her that I'd protect her at all costs and that I was sorry ahead of time for the following screw-ups. She was my second chance at life, with love and opportunity.

When Braylee was 13 weeks old, we faced our first parental obstacle: a health scare. She was diagnosed with a urinary tract infection (UTI). Despite the frustration that came when medical professionals questioned my knowledge of caring for a baby girl, we returned home with antibiotics in hand, only to discover she had yet another UTI weeks later. The following four weeks were a tumultuous sequence of doctor's appointments, persistent fevers, and stubborn infections that antibiotics couldn't resolve. Pushed to the edge and propelled by a mother's instinct, I found the strength to advocate for my daughter, imploring the doctors to consider the possibility of an underlying condition that was evading diagnosis. She was later diagnosed with bilateral bladder Reflux, something we had never heard of. After nearly losing her one night due to a febrile seizure, I called the UVA Pediatric Urology department. I left a tearful voicemail on their machine overnight, desperately begging for help. The following day, a nurse called and asked us to come to UVA immediately with Braylee and her scans. Keep in mind we were only 21 years old. We had absolutely no clue how to care for a sick child, and learning to advocate for her was both exhausting and confusing. I doubted my ability to care for her almost daily, as I couldn't fix her and wasn't sure if anyone could. Fortunately, we had the opportunity to meet with one of the top urologists in the country, who assured us that this was an easy fix but would require surgery. He challenged us to try some medication trials with the hope that she could grow out of it, and if they didn't work, we could opt for surgery. It wasn't even a month later when she had yet another infection that affected her kidneys. With one swift phone call, we were at UVA within a week, handing our 6-month-old baby girl over to a surgeon for a 6-hour surgery.

We were so fortunate the surgery did the trick. After a week in the hospital, we finally brought our baby home and guess what? She slept through the night for the first time! It was amazing to see her little personality start to shine through. We could focus on enjoying the baby experience - watching her crawl, smile, laugh, and babble. Those nights at home, just chilling with kid shows, having simple meals, and being together, were meaningful. We learned so much and grew even closer as a couple. Figuring out how to be an adult, first-time parents, and keep a tiny human alive at such a young age can either make or break you, but we took each day at a time and leaned into each other as much as we could. Bit by bit, I could sense parts of my life and fragments of my heart starting to heal. Maybe not completely, but it was something. Feeling loved, empowered, and like you could shape the future on your terms felt pretty darn good.

What no one prepares you for, however, is the mountain of medical bills that start rolling in after a medical fiasco. From the hospital stays to the labs and the ER visits, there was an endless cycle of new bills arriving daily. Several scans and tests, which our insurance argued against covering, added to an already stressful period. This administrative battle alone is a beast that can consume your everyday life. With both Ryan and I employed in family businesses, we had good jobs, yet the financial strain was palpable. Gratefully, we leaned heavily on our parents' support and the generosity of our church community. Despite the help, we meticulously adhered to the numerous payment plans we had set up.

About a month post-Braylee's surgery, the financial overload pushed me to seek an evening job. I scoured online job listings, searching for part-time work that offered the flexibility and pay we needed. For weeks, I came up empty-handed until I found myself gravitating toward an industry I had never imagined entering: Direct Sales. Growing up, I was super familiar with the industry and what it entailed. I attended a lot of different home parties with my mom and family members, and my mom actively sold one as I was growing up to bring in extra income. I had made it known as a young adult I'd never put my foot in that door, but here I was jumping ship to sink or swim. What I didn't realize was that my decision in the fall of 2007 would change everything about my life and who I was and would unlock a deep desire to figure out my purpose in life. The saga of self-discovery began, and I would spend the next 15 years of my life riding a roller coaster that did not come with a handbook.

Dear Ryan,

As I wrote this chapter, I experienced every emotion from being giddy, excited, sad, fearful and thankful. Our life has been full of moments that embodies each of those specifically. Writing a chapter, dedicated to the start of our life together has filled me with a lot of pride and thankfulness. From the depths of my soul and the corners of my heart, where words often find solace, I write to you. A letter, though simple, carries the weight of our shared laughter, the tears we've wiped away, and the dreams we've dared to dream together. It is an attempt to encapsulate what often remains unsaid but not unfelt within the rhythm of our everyday life, and captured in this book of which has been a dream of mine for years and one you've encouraged me to fulfill.

Reflecting on our journey, walking hand in hand through life and that one time even along the soft, sandy beaches of Hawaii to the thrilling adventure of dog sledding in Montana, each memory we've created is a testament to the unbreakable bond we share. Riding around those dirt roads, with nothing but us, our thoughts, and the world around us, I found freedom. But it was in my moments of vulnerability, like during my first panic attack when you held me so tightly, or the way you looked at me as I gave birth to both of our children that I found safety.

You have been my rock, my safe haven. Saving me from my fears, accepting me in my entirety, and protecting me even when I didn't realize I needed it. You've unfolded before me the very essence of friendship, gratefulness, sincerity, and an unfaltering hope that propels us forward. Your grace in forgiveness, your steadfastness in our faith, and your unwavering support have allowed us both to grow – not just alongside each other, but into the very fabric of one another's being.

Even after 18 years, the anticipation of your return home every evening fills me with an inexplicable joy. It feels just like our first week of being married; the excitement, the longing, and then the fulfillment when I hear your truck approach. Your smile remains my weakness, and yes, we certainly won't mention the effect your backward hat has on me. It's these little things, isn't it? They speak volumes of the incredible friend, husband and father you are - your big heart shining through in every action, every decision. We now reside on the very land where we met, and often as I make my way up the driveway I glance over to the left and remember the night vividly. I told everyone...when you know, you know.

Sometimes, in the quiet moments of the evening as I turn down the house, I find myself staring at your boots by the door. They're not just footwear; they are symbols of the path you walk every day, for us. The thoughts that may crowd your mind, the hands that work tirelessly, and the footsteps that lead you back to me — I think of them, and my heart swells with love and compassion. My only prayer is that each day you're met with safety and grace, just as you have always ensured for us. Ryan, if love is a word, then with you, I've discovered its meaning in every shade and color imaginable. You inspire me to be better, to love harder, and to extend the grace you've so freely given me. Our lives, entwined in the beautiful mess of growing up together, have been the greatest adventure of my life.

I look forward to all the days ahead, the challenges we will face, and the joys we'll discover. With you by my side, I am home.

Wuzz you.

ENOUGH ~ 55

Hope & Ryan
November 2021

Chapter 6

The Unexpected Journey to Success

I acknowledge that most people in my circle share my perspective, but I dare to believe that my book will transcend boundaries and touch the lives of countless women. With audacity and determination, I aspire to make a profound impact on a larger scale. So, give me just a moment as I step onto my makeshift podium; I ask you to heed my words with an open heart and mind. I affirm that Direct Selling and MLM—multi-level marketing—organizations are swaddled in stereotypes and scrutiny, often immediately dismissed or frowned upon. Yet, despite many's strong opinions against this industry, it was my lifeline in a time of need. With Braylee's health concerns and the mounting debts, this unlikely path provided a beacon of hope. So before we proceed, I implore you to look past preconceived notions. The insights and transformations that ensued were as unexpected to me as they might be to you.

I soon discovered this industry is riddled with challenges requiring tenacity and a willingness to navigate its labyrinthine nature. Loops, hoops, and a constant need for understanding — I've encountered them all. The judgment cast by individuals on those deriving an income this way, labeling this career choice with scorn, often betrayed a prejudice I used to share. After more than 16 years on the inside, I've seen the shadows of uncertainty and dubious tactics clouding this field. Yet, it's not all bleak—there exist stellar companies whose sole mission is to impact lives positively. I confess, as a former skeptic who pitied those walking this path, my worldview has been fundamentally reshaped. Now, with an earnest plea for your temporary suspension of judgment, I prepare to descend from my soapbox and delve into this transformative chapter of my life.

In the vast sea of selling options, my criteria was slightly demanding. I hungered for innovation and a product line unfamiliar in my area—one that I could champion with honesty and pride. The thirst for financial freedom was undeniable; aligned with this was the necessity for a product I could wholeheartedly endorse. During a sleep-deprived night, cradling Braylee in my arms, I scrutinized each potential company, weighing their values against my ideals. Eventually, my quest culminated in a bold, perhaps reckless decision. With hope as my ally, I invested in my future by purchasing the enrollment kit for $99 plus shipping and tax. A $107 charge that stretched the limits of our solitary credit card to its brink.

The choice was influenced by more than product lines or profit margins; approach, interest and values would tip the scales. Of all the consultants vying for my partnership, one stood out—not for an aggressive sales pitch but for genuine interest in my story. That interaction marked the turning point, reinforcing my belief in the power of a relationship-driven business. The allure of a company whose foundations were deeply rooted in faith and scripture beckoned me to find my place within a community that strives to walk the talk. In this moment of quiet conviction, I chose to join forces with an organization that seemed to echo my values, trusting that this leap of faith was the key to unlocking new doors of opportunity.

Reflecting on those early days, I had absolutely no idea what I was doing 99% of the time. I floundered to remember the names of the products, often mixing them up, and to my embarrassment, I misquoted prices at my first party—a mistake that almost wiped out my entire commission. Additionally, as someone naturally inclined to introversion, the challenge of initiating conversations and effectively communicating with strangers was daunting. I was propelled out of my comfort zone, embarking on a steep learning curve where every interaction was a lesson in salesmanship and interpersonal skills.

However, I was making money each night I left home and I was genuinely having fun. I challenged myself early on to leave a catalog everywhere I went and intentionally ensured I shared it with everyone I had an interaction with. I approached strangers (with hives all over my neck) and made a point to invite every waitress I met to learn more about my lil' business. Early on in my business, I heard someone say, "It's your responsibility to share, and the customers responsibility to accept or decline." I couldn't take their response personally.

This industry demands a certain level of resilience, and unbeknownst to my critics, I developed that at a young age, so I wasn't about to give them a chance to erode it. More often than not, people showed a genuine interest and love for the products. While hearing no and facing rejection became a normal occurrence, I was fortunate to have a supportive network of friends, family, and an incredible community who provided invaluable support in getting it off the ground. I was making a dent in our medical mountain of bills, and in the chaos of being a young mom, working full-time, and building a sales business, something was happening under the surface that I hadn't entirely realized yet. While I juggled phone calls, party nights, a full-time job and playdates between the mobile office and the diaper bag, I was cultivating perseverance and a knack for multitasking that would become invaluable. The small successes, those tiny victories of a sale here, a new connection there, were slowly but surely laying the groundwork for not just a career, but a newfound confidence that I was on the cusp of something truly transformative.

Beyond the tangible benefits of running my own sales business, I found a sense of personal growth and empowerment to be genuinely impactful. As a young mother, getting lost in the daily chaos of raising a family was challenging enough, but doing that all while building my business, I discovered a passion and drive within myself that I didn't know existed.

I began to notice the inner drive of determination kept pushing me through each day - an essential trait when running a successful business, but also a survival trait I'd embodied years prior. I found myself thankful at times that my life leading up to that point had already instilled an abundance of perseverance, determination, and resilience. So giving up wasn't really an option for me. If my calendar was empty, I sought ways to fill it. If my team was struggling, I buckled down to support them. If I hit a rough patch in the business, I was eager to get on the other side of it. There were many setbacks along the way, but I learned to adapt and find solutions rather than give up. I was determined to make this business work. I made connections when I was scared to. I put myself out there by driving through new towns on the weekends to leave my contact information, and for years I had a vendor event every weekend in the fall and this continued to expand my circle of customers. Most events were in different cities, as I wanted growth in more than just my hometown. I stayed up many late nights driving hours to parties, and pulled countless all-nighters building training plans and education programs for my team. I made calls, sent packets, went door-to-door sometimes and stopped by local businesses every chance I got. I was often uncomfortable, but each time I walked away from one of those uncomfortable experiences I found myself standing a bit taller and feeling more confident with each conversation.

Sometimes, the sound of healing still remained silent, but I felt like I was making progress as I grew up and encountered many situations. Becoming a wife, a mom, and a business owner unlocked new strengths within. Each role came with unique challenges and lessons, silently crafting me into the person I am today. This personal evolution was not marked by fanfare or sudden bursts of enlightenment but by the quiet, daily victories that accumulated over time. The resilience in the face of adversity, the joy in small successes, and the silent strength gained from overcoming hardships composed my melody of healing. I failed to notice the intriguing phenomenon unfolding within me for quite some time. Unbeknownst to me, every party, every meeting, every conference, and every connection I made subtly stirred up a whirlwind of acceptance, appreciation, and self-worth. I was really proud of myself.

One of the greatest blessings I found, was being a part of a more extensive sales network provided me with a fantastic support system. I was able to connect with other consultants and leaders who understood the challenges and joys of running their own businesses. We shared tips, advice, and encouragement, creating a sense of community that I never knew I needed or existed for that matter. This network became a source of motivation and inspiration as we celebrated each other's successes, many of us uniting families and lifting each other up during difficult times regardless if it was in our professional or personal lives.

As I embarked further into my career and began climbing the leadership ladder, a new purpose began to unlock. I'd watched other women in the business earn large paychecks, earn hefty leadership bonuses, free trips and walk the stage and began to wonder, couldn't I do that too? Even seeing their pictures in the catalog, I began to yearn for more for myself. This industry is made up of dreamers and doers and I so desperately wanted to dream bigger than I was. This transformative journey shifted my mindset from "Why me?" to "Why not me?" It was a stark contrast to the old me, the one I used to pity. I felt genuinely connected to something extraordinary and craved more of it. I joined this company at the age of 20, and within four years, I reached the pinnacle of the company career plan, attaining the highest title and earning a six-figure income. I was also the youngest to do so in the company to date. I don't share this to boast but to express my profound pride. I accomplished what many deemed impossible. Despite hearing countless times that I couldn't do it, that it wouldn't last, or that I was "one of those sales girls," I persevered. I loved what I did, and every single day, I woke up with a deep sense of purpose. It wasn't just about the product, the people or the income - it was about purpose. This business had become a mission field for me and over the years, I began to understand that this was what God had called me to do.

In the realm of direct sales, leadership transcends the act of guiding a team. It evolves into an endeavor filled with profound personal and shared experiences. Having had the privilege to witness this first-hand, I've come to realize the true essence of leadership—it's not just about achieving personal success, titles or even income. It's about enabling others to realize their dreams. This realization began to reshape my perspective, transforming leadership into a joyous journey of mutual growth and empowerment.

When I first stepped into a leadership role early in my career, I viewed it through the lens of responsibility and goals. Little did I know, it was the beginning of a much more impactful experience—one that involves witnessing women achieve milestones they once thought were out of reach. From inviting someone to join our business venture and then seeing them celebrate their achievements, be it walking the stage, paying off a credit card, saving for a dream trip, or even managing to keep their power on—the sense of fulfillment is immeasurable.

The beauty of direct sales lies in the ripple effect; one act of belief can set in motion a wave of change. The sense of obligation felt to extend this opportunity to as many as possible wasn't a burden but a beacon of hope, illuminating the path for those seeking change. It's about witnessing the new purpose that unlocks within them, mirroring my own evolution. Through each success story, leadership morphed into a gift that kept on giving, not only empowering others but also enriching my own life. It's a testament to the power of sharing one's story and the collective stories that shape our communal narrative. I wanted to create a space where dreams are not just pursued but realized, where barriers are broken, and potential is unlocked. Each achievement, no matter how big or small, would resonate with a sense of collective triumph. This alone reinforces the belief that leadership is not merely a role but a privilege to uplift and inspire.

Therefore, the essence of leadership in direct sales is not encapsulated in the results at the end of the month or the accolades one receives. Instead, it is found in the moments of genuine connection and the ability for lives to be completely transformed.

In a world where the traditional paths often lead us to glass ceilings and closed doors, direct sales and network marketing emerge not just as opportunities but as gateways to a life of unlimited potential. For many, including myself, this opportunity was more than just a job; it became a lifeline. It unlocked a hidden purpose, provided financial freedom, and allowed us to be part of something bigger than ourselves—a community driven by passion, empowerment, and an unshakeable belief in each other's success.

To those who doubt or misunderstand the value of what we do, know this: the direct-selling industry, specifically party-plan, is built on the foundation of fairness, where everyone has an equal shot at success. The only limits are those we place on ourselves. If we find ourselves boxed in, it's a sign that we need to expand our circles and reach even further. At an event one time, I had someone say to me, "No wonder you were successful, you got in at the right time." I smiled and simply replied, "I got in at my right time, when God opened the door, I ran in." I know that being one of the first in area to promote a product may seem ideal, ground floor baby. However, I'll be the first to say that was challenging. Ground floor isn't easy. Instead of just selling a product you love, you have to convince people to trust your brand, your product and yourself. Plus, the growing pains of a new company can be challenging as well. I truly don't believe there is a "right" time to join a company, only "your" right time.

I've faced skepticism, negativity, and direct criticism for choosing this path. While it's easy to focus on the detractors, I've always chosen instead to concentrate on the lives we were and continue to change, including my own. I've heard the whispers of doubt, only to drown them out with the roaring success of those around me living their best lives through the same opportunities that were once ridiculed.

As I scroll social media and see that there are legit trends bashing this industry and the women that choose them, it's disheartening to see division. Especially among women, in a space that should be empowering us all. Choosing a career in direct sales or network marketing is a valid and valuable pursuit friends. Criticism, whether intentional or not, doesn't just hurt; it hinders progress. It's a form of bullying that has no place in our professional discourse or personal interactions. If you don't understand it, that's fine. If you'd never choose it, that's fine. But know this -

Your words DO matter.

That mom who used her last $107 to start a business that she prays will impact her household budget needs a woman like you to cheer her on. Notice I didn't say she needs to you to shop- because if you don't want her product, then there is no need to buy it. However, *you can choose to clap for her.* Share her posts. Celebrate her milestones. Whether you are friends, family, or just social acquaintances, remember kindness is free, and support goes a long way.

I'm aware that some businesses, some companies, and even some consultants make decisions that can damage our reputation - but they don't speak for us all.

This message isn't just a defense—it's a call to action. So when you see a friend, a family member, or even a stranger sharing their product, celebrating a milestone, or simply being passionate about their work, take a moment to support them. Your encouragement might be the fuel they need to keep pushing forward. Furthermore, if the opposite happens and you see them struggling or their company going through a rough patch, be respectful and supportive. It's not a chance to prey, poach, or even say, "I told you so."

Each of us is striving to build a life of meaning and success, however we define it. Instead of pulling each other down, let's lift each other up. Celebrate each triumph, no matter how small it may seem. Remember, in a. world where we can be anything, be kind, be supportive, and most importantly, be for each other's dreams.

To my fellow direct sales and network marketing professionals: hold your heads high. We are trailblazers, building paths for others to follow, paths that lead to empowerment, independence, and success on our own terms. Protect your circle; it's okay to unfollow, remove, or step away from individuals or circles that don't serve you in the season you are in. Remember, the impact we make today will echo in the lives of many tomorrows. Don't spend all of your time trying to convince your friends or family; if this is a chapter God has called you to walk into, and you see an open door, RUN THROUGH IT, SISTER.

I *think* I may have stepped back on my makeshift podium for a moment.....
But, stay with me.

As my journey continued, I achieved what I ultimately wanted. I earned the promotions and the bonuses, found financial success, and traveled across the map with earned trips. I walked that stage, had my moment in the catalog and achieved many goals along the way. Perhaps though, what was happening on the inside, that few could see is what I was most thankful for. The one thing I didn't have on my "vision board". My heart was mending more each moment and little by little, I was discovering that the past learnings and trials I had faced had prepared me for those moments. I basked in self-discovery with each opportunity, seeing that I was strong and worthy of success. I had always envisioned this hole inside my heart, yet through an incredible circle of support—my husband, my family, and my tribe within the business—it was slowly filling up. The pain and disvalue never indeed left, but I could feel myself standing taller and prouder, in control of my destiny.

I of course encountered setbacks, but at the end of the day, my success and the pride I derived from that experience cannot be taken away. This chapter of my life brought healing in ways I never imagined and quite honestly wasn't even looking for. What began as a risk to earn extra income turned into a venture that ignited purpose and vitality within me. We were more than just a company, a team, or consultants. The thought of putting it all into words overwhelms me. I personally witnessed lives being transformed at our team retreats as individuals found solace in their peers and the ministry of our company, even leading some to Christ for the first time. I helped a young girl escape a toxic relationship by guiding her finances discreetly and supporting her transition to a new apartment for a fresh start. I've experienced heartache, holding another woman as she grieved the loss of her child or embarking on a 14-hour road trip to be by the side of a fellow leader after her second child was diagnosed with cancer. We were a family, and I took immense pride in protecting it. I still yearn for others to discover similar opportunities. There are communities, tribes, and women who are not merely waiting to see if you succeed before they lean into you, but are genuinely there for you through thick and thin.

Over the years, I slowly regained my voice. Feeling proud of myself was a new experience and I started to love myself and, more importantly, forgive myself. My family was proud of me, my husband was proud of me, and I was proud of myself. From broken to whole, from silent to outspoken, my journey was not just about building a business; it was about rediscovering my own strength and worth. This transformation echoed in every aspect of my life, repairing relationships and establishing new ones on foundations of mutual respect and admiration.

I am forever grateful for the lessons I learned as a national leader in the Direct Sales Industry. They were not just business lessons but personal ones as well. I knew the true value of community and how it can shape our lives in ways we never imagined. Through my experiences, I have discovered that success is not just about achieving financial or career goals. It's truly about finding purpose and fulfillment in our lives. It is about surrounding ourselves with people who lift us up and support us personally and professionally, no matter the season.

As women, we are often taught to compete against each other, but I have seen the power of collaboration and support firsthand. When we unite and lift each other up, there is no limit to what we can achieve. This is why I am dedicated to mentoring and supporting other women in the business world, helping them realize their full potential and break through any barriers that may hold them back.

My time as a leader in this industry was a true gift and continues to impact me daily. I have grown and evolved in ways I never thought possible. I have always felt this direct sales opportunity was the vehicle God used to help me find healing, restoration, and, more than anything, purpose. I began to develop a hunger, desire, and pull to help other women own their stories and discover self-worth, so the mission grew with each day. It was more than just products, sales, and growth. It was about impact. I remember someone telling my husband that everything would crumble one day, just to wait and see, and he replied with, "Well, we'll ride that train until it stops, proudly." We knew we were a part of something bigger than us, and we saw firsthand the impact it was having on us and others around us. We took each step in faith and anytime we saw God crack a door open, we ran right through it.

As I connected with individuals on my journey, I began speaking for other teams in the company and even in the industry. Each connection was an opportunity to share my success story, and the inspiration to ignite others to believe and chase their dreams. When asked, I was candid about how this business had changed my life and transformed me into a different person, but I guarded my past closely, afraid to unveil the doors that held the depth of my transformational progress to date.

I'd made a lot of progress, endured a lot, and achieved a lot in the few years I'd been in the business, and I did, in fact, make it to the top. What I didn't expect was the season of life that would come right when I made it there. As someone who likes to be in control and plan out my life, I wasn't prepared for the season approaching in 2010 that would allow my inner demons to triumph over what remained of my vulnerabilities, that would cause me to unravel.

Chapter 7

Confronting the Pain Within

As you dive deeper into my story, the pace of transformation from early hardships to ultimate success might feel like a movie. The middle of this tale hits a turning point where you might pause and reflect: the journey from a challenging childhood and teenage years to the seismic shift of becoming a mother and achieving professional greatness. It's like each chapter builds on the previous one, leading to a powerful and, honestly, somewhat sudden climax. This realization of becoming an inspiration overshadowed the quieter, gradual steps of my journey, leaving you curious about the inner workings of such a transformation if you only heard the bits of the stories I chose to share for years. While there is a lifetime of pain behind me, my journey toward success and finding my voice has been shaped by everything I've encountered and experienced. While not a simple path, it's my path.

For years, I was consumed by the hustle, always charging ahead yet neglecting to understand myself fully. At a young age, my nanny told me I was unique, special, and intricately crafted by God. However, I never allowed myself the freedom to question my own identity as I grew up. For nearly 25 years, I had been in straight survival mode. I had experienced a lifetime filled with changes, pain, abuse, fear, rejection, some joys, significant losses, and overwhelming memories that I often blocked and refused to face. Life was like a fast-moving train and it didn't make many stops, oftentimes leading me to not deal with my feelings or emotions.

By the age of 14, I'd had three fathers in my life: one who shared my blood but appeared content without me, one who wanted to choose me but couldn't, another I'd rather forget, and three families—some of which felt like brief encounters. I had nearly ten relocations and various living situations by this time, as well as a taxing relationship that aged me prematurely and left me hollow, resulting in decisions I regret as I would try to pursue love and acceptance. Then, at 15, a new chapter with a new dad, new home, and new family would eventually lead me to meet my husband. By 19, I was married. At 20, I became a mom and started a side hustle that, within a few years, turned into a million-dollar business.

I often reflect and see a lifetime of events that transpired within just the first two decades of my life. Never once was there really a moment I was forced to face it intimately. Head down, keep hustling. Keep surviving. Keep moving.

So, as I continued to drive fast through life and began to reach the peak of my career, at times it felt like time I was sometimes an observer. I found it difficult to be in the moment and truly embrace the seasons of transformation that had occurred. I do believe healing and transformation were occurring to an extent, but I'd never even once slowed down enough to really be honest with myself about my past, the trauma I carried, and the debilitating nightmares and fears that still riddled my mind.

As I mentioned earlier, sometimes you have to face the harsh realities of life. If you don't, those locked and buried boxes will eventually resurface. For some, this comes through growing up, therapy, self-reflection, counseling, and prayer....and for some, it occurs when you lose control. So, when I say that the fall of 2010 caught me off guard, it's an understatement. I was never prepared for or anticipated the profound and overwhelming depression that would engulf me after the birth of my second child, Austin. After experiencing a smooth pregnancy and delivery, which was quite different from my first child, I welcomed home a flawless baby with a good appetite, who slept peacefully and was simply perfect.

Just a week or so after his birth, I found myself with a heaviness in my chest I had never entirely experienced before. Panic began to set in, and no matter what I tried, the pain continued. Each of our parents was over that night for supper, and I remember sitting on the nursery floor, trying to convince myself it was not there. However, it continued, and after a quick call to the doctor, we made our way to the Emergency Room. Snagging a kiss from Braylee and one of those deep inhales of my newborn's smell, I left in tears, unsure of what was about to unfold.

A few hours later, the cardiologist's words seemed robotic as they came out, like a haunting echo that carried the weight of an uncertain future. As he explained the implications, my thoughts battled between fear and disbelief. The sound of shuffling papers and the click of his pen provided a backdrop to a world that suddenly looked different with this grim diagnosis. I found myself in a new reality where every heartbeat felt like a countdown, bringing me closer to the moments I might miss with my children growing up without me. With a cold tone, this doctor told us about my diagnosis and what it meant. He explained that even with treatment, I could expect to live for 7-9 years based on my stage of diagnosis. His direct tone and lack of concern or empathy made me instantly believe he was confident and determined to get the point across.

Pulmonary Hypertension wasn't just a medical term; it was a thief in the night, stealing the years I had hoped to fill with love, laughter, and the unexpected adventures of life.

To say I was devastated is an understatement. I returned home with fear riddling my bones, a nearly tangible shiver that wouldn't cease. I was just shy of 25 years old, cradling two babies in my arms, with a career that I had finally gotten to the top of. I wasn't done, though; I had plans. I wanted more. My life was supposed to blossom, not be inching towards an untimely wilting. A follow-up visit was hastily scheduled, replete with plans for a heart catheterization and advice for managing blood pressure. However, those following nights were not spent in pursuit of rest or recovery. Like so many before me, I turned to the glow of an internet screen, scouring page after page for an inkling of hope amidst the relentless prognosis of misery and morbidity that awaited me. My blood pressure was the least of my concerns, eclipsed by the overbearing dread of an uncertain and seemingly doomed future. Each new article, each statistic, was like another shovel of dirt on the grave of my former life—paralysis set in, not of the body, but of the soul. I watched my children laugh and play, a specter at the feast of life, unable to partake. The doctor's words, cold yet confident, had struck a blow that left me reeling, unable to reconcile the reality of my diagnosis with the years I thought lay ahead.

We went in for the heart catheterization a few weeks later. Austin was about five weeks old then, and I can vividly recount how that morning unfolded. The grip of fear was unyielding as I wrestled with the impending reality that might unfold post-test. My prayers were fervent, a cascade of pleas to a power more significant than the maladies that bound my health. As we made our way into the cardiology unit, an unexpected yet comforting sight—my pastor, his presence unsolicited, was there standing sentinel. He had been a stalwart figure in my life, and in that moment, his grasp on my hands and the prayer we shared provided an anchor in the whirlwind of my nervousness. The time arrived for me to be prepped, clad in a hospital gown, the physical proof of recent motherhood trickling down my stomach. A nurse briefed us on the procedures, promising the doctor would visit shortly to finalize preparations.

The doctor who entered, however, was a stranger. My usual physician had been called away, and in his place stood this new custodian of my case, who introduced himself with a calm demeanor that belied the moment's gravity. After initial niceties and a brief examination, my plight as a recent mother seemed to arrest his medical intuition. He studied my chart with a furrowed brow, his line of questioning targeted and acute. Decision draped in his expression, he emerged from contemplation with a verdict that seemed unthinkable; he suspected that Pulmonary Hypertension, the ghoul that had stalked my nightmares, was a misdiagnosis. As a new mother, my heart had suffered, indeed, but he believed what I needed was time for natural recovery, not the invasive exploration of heart catheterization. I didn't have the symptoms that came with the diagnosis. I'd encountered sensations the night I landed in the ER, and he wasn't convinced the scans proved anything more than a fleet of anxiety as a new mom. This physician—I had just met— wished to take the mantle of my care, to understand the nuances of my condition with patience and scrutiny.

Thus, as I left the hospital that day, it was with lungs that I finally tasted the sweetness of hope; as just before that appointment, my pastor had prayed that we might walk in that day and learn of a misdiagnosis and be graced with a doctor who listened beyond the heartbeat he was trained to hear. My heart, burdened with the labor of life-giving, needed respite, not further challenge. And at that moment, the truth of prayers given wings revealed itself, not just in the certainty that I might live without the forecasted affliction, but in the affirmation that sometimes, the answers to our most fervent pleas sit quietly in the hands of those who choose to listen.

I wish I could say I flipped a switch and moved on, but the entire situation amplified every whisper of my body until whispers sounded like alarms. My mind became a carousel of fixation, frantically spiraling each time a new symptom appeared, always jumping to the worst conclusions. Seeking the dubious counsel of the internet became my daily ritual—a readily woven web of anxiety that ensnared me helplessly. There I sat, ensconced in uncertainty, even as I shuffled through countless appointments and endured the cold embrace of heart monitors and the rhythmic drumming of EKGs. I was in a ceaseless countdown to the six-month scan that promised confirmation or reprieve. Anxiety, an unfamiliar demon until this season, began to daily sink its claws deep, driving me into a frenzy of fear so pervasive that I struggled to find joy or maintain focus. Moments that should have been filled with living were stolen by the specter of what might be. Try as I might, snapping out of this dreaded cycle seemed impossible.

My 6-month scan came back, and by the grace of God, whether it was due to healing or the ER doctor's incorrect but cold diagnosis, I was cleared of the condition. I did have a benign heart murmur, but that was it. The doctor thought that the chest pain and symptoms I experienced were actually from anxiety, you know, adjusting to having two kids instead of one. Little did he know, my body was, unfortunately, getting used to being overridden with anxiety since that first night in the ER. I was grateful, no lousy prognosis, and I came home hopeful. I was determined to get a handle on my emotions and life. This situation had consumed me for six months, completely paralyzing me. Early on, it triggered postpartum anxiety and depression, things I had never dealt with before. While life was moving forward and my business was growing, the loud and intense screams of frustration and anxiety were still in my soul.

I just wanted to cry out, to escape my body and go back to a more genuine version of myself.

This entire episode activated a season for me that I had absolutely no control of. I was constantly enveloped in anxiety, and the depression originally started as a fear of dying and leaving my family. Eventually, it eroded to the point where I questioned if I truly deserved the life I was building and began dealing with thoughts and emotions I didn't have control over. Nightmares of my childhood woke me many nights, leaving me fearful to even rest at times. I felt very defensive and misunderstood, and I started questioning everyone's motives around me, taking things way too personally, and just wanting to hide in my little cocoon. In one of the lowest points of my adult life, as I was fighting for my life emotionally and mentally, I unexpectedly faced another chapter of change that came on the other side of my medical mishap—one that nearly shattered me and only furthered the depression to a level that almost destroyed me and everything I had.

It was a challenge I had never anticipated nor prepared for. At one point, I didn't think I could handle anything else, but the joke was on me as I was confronted with a season of anguish, betrayal, and anger. Remember those boxes I kept buried? Well, that "daddy issues" box, the one I had neatly stowed away, resurfaced as if on a magical carpet right before my eyes.

Chapter 8

The Unraveling of Fragile Threads

My parents have always been and will always be some of the most influential people in my life. Seeing my mom happy, finally in a home that felt right, filled my heart with joy. What was even more incredible was gaining a new dad who had become "MY dad." These are my parents - not because of blood, but because they choose to be every single day. Since meeting him around the age of 14, there was never a moment of doubt that this man was created to be my dad. I proudly carried his name as my own, and to make it even better, they lived just a quick 10-minute drive away, making them a big part of our daily lives.

One evening, when my mom was visiting with the kids and playing with Braylee while Austin, still an infant, lay nearby, she dropped a bombshell - she and my dad were getting a divorce. I was absolutely shattered. Battling postpartum issues, already heavily influenced by the medical scare, had me in a constant state of being fragile, and hearing those words made me crumble. It honestly felt like a betrayal, even though it wasn't about me. For years, my children had seen my current dad as my only dad, shielded from the idea of separation. The news shattered the decade of stability, love, and present parenting we had encountered, and I couldn't understand why this was an option. I remember staring blankly at her as tears filled my eyes, thoughts racing to make sense of what she had just said. What in the world?

In the past, when divorce shadowed our family, we lost connections with one side, and though I wasn't particularly saddened by it, this situation did scare me. It terrified me actually. This chapter of our lives holds much complexity, but their divorce isn't my tale to share. Ultimately, I can only express how it impacted me and what transpired. I can say it felt like the ground beneath me crumbled with each step and this trial would trigger my anxiety and depression to an entirely new level and undo a lot of what had been put back together over the years.

At some point, possibly due to my inclination to control situations, I found myself serving as a mediator for them. In hindsight, it was unwise for both of them to presume that of me or to allow it. I openly advocated for their marriage to be restored, and I thought about it daily. It's unhealthy for a child, regardless of age, to be entangled in conversations and decisions like this. Yet, for someone like me, somewhat silently battling anxiety and depression, I began losing grip day by day. I always prided myself on being very self-aware and adept at recognizing the onset of anxiety or discussing my depression. Still, nevertheless, with time slipping away, I found myself increasingly unable to reign in my thoughts and responses. Thankfully, my husband adeptly shielded and supported me, recognizing the toll that assuming the role of full-time mediator was taking on our marriage, parenting, and business. Depression can coax you into believing you are isolated and misunderstood, prompting me to withdraw from connections, and he could see I was drifting into a dark hole. I felt stifled and I was losing my grasp on things.

Threads that once intertwined me with some of the most influential people in my life became fragile right before my eyes. And honestly, I didn't have the strength or desire to take action sometimes. During this season of my life, I admittedly look back and realize how much I pulled myself away from people I cared about. I retreated to a safe place within my mind where I felt no one could access me so that they couldn't hurt or trigger my fears. I was often frustrated that others didn't feel like me or understand me. I felt alone, abandoned almost. One of the final straws for me was losing one of my closest friends of over a decade. After a family member of hers reached out following a significant loss in their family, asking I give her some space to be with her family and allow them to heal together. I actually did understand this; it was a unique situation, and my loyalty to her had me right smack dab in the middle of it all daily. I wanted to be there for her and be a friend, but I respected the request. What started as me stepping back for a few days suddenly turned into weeks and then months, and our friendship slowly faded away. I remember wondering how long it would take her to reach out, but she didn't, and I began to fear that maybe it was best that I step away. Reflecting on it, I regret not fighting to hold on, and even today, I wonder if stepping back was a mistake on my part. I convinced myself the friendship may have been one-sided since she didn't come looking for me, but due to my current state of mind and emotions, I just let it go. At the time, dealing with my challenges and mindset, I found myself retreating even further, and the decision was, unfortunately, easy for me at the end of it all. My love for her and her family led me to believe this was the best thing for her. It remains a loss I mourn, even now. Back then, even as supportive as my husband was, he was beginning to see those unopened boxes surface as I began to fight demons and past hurts in my most vulnerable state to date. I'm sure he was questioning many things and probably praying for a life preserver.

He navigated our tumultuous waters with tenderness and steadfastness I hadn't fully appreciated until much later. Amidst the turmoil, I realized just how profound an impact unaddressed trauma can have. It waits, like a silently ticking time bomb, until the pressures of life trigger an explosion of pain and confusion. Slowly but surely, the boxes begin to open, revealing past traumas buried deep within. I found myself growing resentful of my parents for giving up so quickly and treating their divorce as if it were insignificant. I became scared of losing my dad, my step-siblings, and his entire family. Why would he continue to assume that role when he was no longer obligated to? I was filled with anguish at the thought of losing him. Additionally, I felt frustrated with my mom, as I failed to comprehend why she wasn't willing to allow more time before finalizing the decision.

Even as an adult with my own family, I began to feel incredibly lonely, and the strong bonds that once brought healing, stability, and restoration began. There is a recurring pattern of choices in my history that may come as a shock to some before now, but as I have shared these stories and unfolded them on these pages, it should come as no surprise that my mom has been married multiple times, resulting in divorce each time. I won't dwell on this topic for long, as it is her personal journey. However, the majority of my story is to share how each of these marriages impacted me as an individual and shaped my life. It is important to note that I love my mom with every fiber of my being. She has been a constant presence, my best friend, and has always been there for me. Even during seasons of challenge, I have never truly questioned if she'd be there for me. That said, it wasn't until I emerged from my own introspection and healing process that I discovered something profound. Everyone responds to trauma differently. Sometimes, unwise decisions are made out of fear or the need for self-preservation and provision. As an adult, I became aware that my mom was on her journey of healing and forgiveness, addressing past traumas that she had experienced all the way from a child to an adult. I only wish she had embarked on this path sooner because we've talked at length often about how she has spent a lifetime running from her past, and through many conversations, I know she has a long list of decisions she wishes she could undo. Ultimately, what happened happened, and over the years as you'll learn, I began to identify the generational cycles that may continue if I didn't make a decision to break them.

What we choose to do with our experiences is up to us individually. Witnessing another marriage falling apart and another family's bonds coming undone was tricky and painfully familiar. Since I had not fully healed myself at this time, it triggered deep-seated fears of failure, neglect, being forgotten, and questioning my worthiness of genuinely being loved as a daughter. All too familiar fears eroded my heart, leading me to make a series of nonsensical decisions that kept me running away from the life I had built and desired. Instead, I found myself in a place of destruction, convinced I did not deserve stability and happiness.

I began to distance myself from Ryan, my husband, who had shared a lifetime's worth of moments with me. Suddenly, I felt inadequate, as if he deserved someone better than me, someone who was not so broken. Reflecting on my past, I wondered if I should have chosen a partner who was equally damaged. Amid depression, trauma, and fear, it became difficult to relate to others who seemed unaffected. Ryan had never indeed witnessed my moments of confusion and doubt, nor had he experienced the pain of divorce and a fractured family. He only knew who I had become after overcoming some of those challenges or at least putting them behind me. As I continued this painful but familiar road, I gradually closed myself off from him. Our home became a place of arguments, blame, and emptiness. Simple things triggered my anxiety, and I struggled to connect with my children, especially my daughter. I was in pain, consumed by loneliness. At that time, I felt like a mere shell of a person, going through the motions of running my business, being a mother, and caring for the house, but feeling empty inside. The sudden upheaval in our family dynamic had shaken me to my core, unleashing all my fears and overshadowing the quiet life I had built. I felt like a child again. Helpless.

If you have ever battled depression, one of the most common sensations, I think, is numbness. That was the best way to describe how I felt daily. I was numb to everything around me. I remember instances where Ryan would plead with me to talk, pray together, or seek professional help, and the normal me would have buckled after one ask. I loved this man with every ounce of my soul, but I honestly questioned if this was the life I was supposed to live and whom I was supposed to share it with. I felt he deserved so much better, and honestly, I played a blame game for a while. He didn't understand or know how to help me, making me resent him. It's crazy to me to look back at some of this, but it was my reality. I was in the pit of despair, and my trauma response was to destroy it all. I was not worthy of normalcy, and that is so incredibly sad to me now that I felt this way. Being a believer and knowing God my entire life wasn't enough for me during this season. I felt God had turned his back on me. I questioned my faith and the God I was taught to serve that I thought loved me. The one who would protect and be there for me. I felt like He had dropped the ball on all of those promises.

Do you ever hear stories like this, the before and after of a life lived and wonder if there is a defining moment that turned the tide for them? I do; I always wonder what made someone go get help, or who tore down their walls, or at what moment it all became visible that they needed to make a change. For me, there was a significant moment when I started to turn the page, but what fueled me each day was this overwhelming yearning to be acknowledged, listened to, and understood. Deep down, despite the pain, I longed for recovery. I wanted to break free from this. I was still aware that living this way wasn't what I wanted. And then, over time, a series of events unfolded, gradually granting me a newfound self-awareness. It allowed me to see my situation externally, like looking through a different lens. Now, you might expect me to say that I sought therapy and began taking care of myself, but I invite you to visualize this season of my life as I experienced it.

I felt like I had been dropped into a dark cave, with only a tiny sliver of light shining from above. I secluded myself in a corner of that dimly lit space, hidden from view, curling up and burying my head in my knees. While a few courageous individuals ventured into the darkness with me to engage in conversation, most seemed to be standing over me, waiting for me to either crumble or rise. Yet, neither of those scenarios unfolded. Instead, I found myself retreating to that corner, shielding my heart from the world. I sat there, gently rocking back and forth, earnestly pleading with a God I knew existed to reveal Himself to me. I yearned for His guidance in discovering happiness and love once more. I longed for Him to demonstrate His care for me and help me comprehend why I never had a father figure in my life, why my mother suffered divorce after divorce, and why my sister and I repeatedly experienced family losses. I questioned why I endured neglect and abuse as a child, why my biological father didn't love or search for me, why a man could subject me to abuse, and ultimately, why I even existed. I dwelled in that secluded corner for an eternity, nearly losing everything. My marriage and my business were on the brink of explosion.

Yet, let us continue the vision together. Picture God entering that faint glow of light, standing beneath it with His hand extended towards me. Imagine Him calling my name, only for me to stubbornly keep my gaze lowered, hoping that by remaining motionless, I could evade further pain. This image vividly represents the essence of that chapter in my life. I, huddled in the dark corner, the Lord standing beneath the feeble ray of light, reaching out to me. However, it required not only my movement but also the strength to rise and grasp His hand. At the time, I didn't feel capable or deserving of approaching Him. I also was frustrated with Him.

But then God.

He moved instead. He moved first.

My mom and sister started attending a new church during this time, and they invited us to join them one Sunday. Admittedly, we hadn't been regular churchgoers for a few months; amidst my struggles and the feeling of betrayal from a God I'd known all my life, I wasn't too concerned about my faith at the time. What had been a priority most of my life was something I was struggling to maintain or even desire. However, with Ryan's persistence, we went.

The moment we stepped into the church, we were welcomed with the familiar vibe of what we call "holy rollers"—a good old-fashioned Pentecostal atmosphere, so we were comfortable from the start. As we settled into our seats—black metal chairs in the right corner of the building—the service began with a guest speaker. I don't remember the message, but as the service ended and we bowed our heads for prayer during the altar service, it exuded a sense of tradition for me and felt comforting.

As the altar began to fill up with members seeking refuge, I couldn't help but notice the familiar sight - a hallmark of Pentecostal churches. If you've ever witnessed the fervor of prayer or experienced the humbling act of falling on your face at the altar, you understand the indescribable liberation it brings. Deep down, I yearned to rush to the front, but being a guest there, I wasn't comfortable taking the first step. Instead, I silently prayed, asking God to soften my soul, to grant me the ability to hear His voice once more, and to reassure me of His presence.

What happened next will forever be ingrained into my soul for eternity.

Returning to the microphone, the preacher requested that everyone close their eyes again. He revealed that the Lord was compelling him, urging him to connect with someone present in the room. I'm sharing this verbatim, but most of his words still echo vividly in my mind.

"There is a young lady in here looking for a father. She's been hurt, forgotten, confused, and betrayed by her own father and the many who assumed that role. Child, listen up. Daughter of the King, pay attention. Your daddy is right here. No earthly father will ever live up to the Heavenly one that is waiting for you to run into His arms. He will never leave or forsake you, and He sees you, sister. He sees you cannot stand up. He sees you cannot move. He wants you to know He's not waiting on you, too; He wants to pick you up. Rest in His arms. You are a daughter of the King. One He chose, One He loves, and He has a plan for you. Give it up; it's time to let Him love you."

Yeah.....

This was the first time I had experienced something quite like it. So, you can imagine that moment's profound impact on my life. I didn't even have to move because God lifted me and carried me toward the light. It was a moment of realization, as I had hit rock bottom and made regrettable choices, hurting my husband with hurtful words and decisions, that I felt deep remorse as the light touched my face. I became acutely aware of the pain I had caused in our marriage and our future, and on the nights that followed, I was faced with a reflection of the entire year that had negatively consumed our lives.

Emotions surged within me as I recognized the distance I had traveled from solace. I understood how deeply my trauma response had affected the ones I loved, especially the ones who loved me the most. Through prayer, discussion, guidance, and forgiveness, we embarked on a journey of recovery and restoration. I leaned into therapy and recommitted myself to God and His purpose for me to still be here.

As much as I would love to tie this dark chapter of my life with a neat bow and move on, I have come to understand the importance of facing the consequences of burying the past. The process of unraveling tightly wound threads is painful, scary, and even paralyzing. At that moment, I truly felt that my Savior, my Heavenly Father, had rescued me from that cave. For the first time, I felt chosen and cherished as a daughter. Finding peace and redemption, I accepted Him as my father and delved into prayer and study.

During this season, both Ryan and I grew significantly. It was not a smooth process, but looking back, we realize we are better individuals because of everything. While we would never want to relive those moments or wish them upon anyone else, they were integral to my healing journey. It took hitting rock bottom and opening all the boxes to reach this point. The unraveling process stripped me down to my core, exposing all the pain, affliction, and battle wounds that I had so effectively hidden for years. It also revealed my progress in tapping into my inner strength and inspiration, urging me to let her free once again. I wanted more for my life.

It just took me a while to realize that I actually deserved it.

The realization that bonds, once held unshakeable, were fraying at the edges stirred a mix of disbelief and urgency within me. It was like my eyes were opened, and I realized I was breathing in an atmosphere thick with tension, a prelude to the storm that threatened to wash away the trust and camaraderie that had taken years to cultivate. It became clear that to weather this storm, action was needed—to mend what was torn and reinforce the connections before they broke completely. This chapter of my life demanded resilience and a commitment to open, honest dialogue. I began to extend olive branches, strain to listen even when it hurt, share my true thoughts with my parents, and share my vulnerabilities in hopes of mutual understanding. It was challenging to navigate the complexities of human emotions and the histories that shaped them, but acknowledging the effort was a part of the healing. Every conversation was an attempt to knit the unraveled threads back together, to salvage a tapestry of relationships that formed the backdrop of my existence.

As I continued on this journey, I learned to embrace vulnerability and the power of authentic communication. Through these difficult conversations, true healing and growth could occur. I found strength in my relationships and a newfound sense of self-worth by facing my fears and opening up about my struggles.

It wasn't just about repairing broken bonds but also building stronger ones. I began to invest more time and effort into cultivating healthy relationships with those who uplifted and supported me. I surrounded myself with individuals who shared my values and encouraged me to be the best version of myself.

This process taught me to set boundaries and prioritize my well-being. I did not need to explain myself or my goals to everyone around me, this was about me. I realized that I needed to first take care of myself to maintain healthy relationships. This meant saying no to toxic behaviors and situations and prioritizing self-care practices.

Looking back on this chapter of my life, I am grateful for this season. Undoubtedly one of the hardest, but it was the launching pad for discovering who I was. As well as who I was meant to be, allowing myself to be genuinely loved versus running away and taking the first step at true healing and restoration. Navigating these challenges helped me gain a deeper understanding of myself and those around me.

Chapter 9

Reclaiming the Reins

As I embarked on what I consider the other side of the mountain, a new season of change and a sincere season of healing and forgiveness, I embarked on intensive therapy. This therapy journey was a deliberate step toward reclaiming my narrative. Through the guidance of a skilled therapist, I began peeling back the layers of my past, confronting the stories I had told myself that no longer served me. It was a profound process that required courage and commitment, and with each session, I felt a greater sense of empowerment and clarity. I won't deny that it was hard and some sessions felt like I'd been turned inside out. Therapy provided me with a safe space to understand and reshape my narrative, transforming my perceived weaknesses into sources of strength.

But therapy is just one tool in the journey towards empowerment. Another crucial aspect is learning to identify and address toxic behaviors and situations in our lives. This can include setting boundaries, standing up for ourselves, and removing ourselves from harmful environments or relationships.

It may also involve recognizing and addressing unhealthy behavior patterns, such as people-pleasing or self-sabotage.

Owning our narrative also means recognizing the power of vulnerability and embracing it in our relationships. When we let go of the need to appear perfect or invulnerable, we open ourselves to deeper connections and authentic communication. This vulnerability may initially feel uncomfortable, but the rewards of meaningful connections are well worth it.

Rebuilding the friendship and love between my husband required consistent and daily effort. We embraced a new level of understanding, delving into more profound and genuine emotions. He became more acquainted with every part of me, from untold stories of my past to my present struggles, while always supporting my journey. Living with regret for falling into that dark place became a daily burden, but he reminded me that acknowledging the path that led me there was crucial and that progress awaited each new day. Therapy became the catalyst for realizing that I wasn't "crazy" or irreparably damaged; instead, I carried a heavy load of past trauma, pain, and fear that influenced my responses to life's challenges. The intense emotions of fear, pain, and a sense of losing control considerably influenced how I responded to significant life events. These included a life-altering medical scare, the challenges of welcoming a second child, and the uncharted journey of motherhood, all while navigating the aftermath of my parents' divorce.

The journey of self-discovery and growth is ongoing, requiring constant effort to maintain a healthy sense of self. It also involves acknowledging that we are human and will make mistakes. We must take responsibility when we make a mistake, apologize if necessary, and learn from the experience.

In addition to owning our narrative and taking responsibility for our actions, we must surround ourselves with a supportive community. Whether it's family, friends, church or a therapist, having a solid support system is essential in navigating life's challenges and maintaining mental wellness.

I immersed myself in my career, looking towards the future. Slowly, I began to rebuild the connections with each of my parents, carefully navigating the delicate balance between blame and misunderstanding. It wasn't my responsibility to mend them or fully grasp their differences. The only aspect I could influence was my relationship with each of them. It dawned on me that if I wanted my dad to remain a constant presence in my life, I also had to put in the effort to nurture that connection. While I will always grieve for what could have been, I have also come to terms with it. I learned to cherish, listen, and savor our shared moments in this chapter. I had diligently cultivated these relationships, even during the challenging times, because I was confident that my parents loved me and that my dad would always be there for me and my children.

My therapist challenged me to focus on what drives me; work was my passion; I excelled at it and knew it was my calling. So, each day, I challenged myself to explore new horizons and gradually ease my way back into my business. I vividly remember a late-night meeting with my leaders, where I humbly apologized for my absence and the season of stillness I had experienced. In that vulnerable moment, I expressed deep gratitude for their friendship and the space they had graciously given me. It was a chapter of depression that had consumed me, but these incredible women, scattered across the globe, never once left my side. They kept things afloat when I lacked the energy or desire. They rallied around me, lifting me. Some even sent me a daily scripture each morning, serving as a source of inspiration. We collaborated, igniting brainstorming sessions and reigniting the flame that once burned inside me.

I always had a deep urge to use my business for something greater than just selling products and making money. But I could never quite put my finger on it. Over the years, I naturally connected with countless women and their stories. I discovered that being a source of inspiration and believing in someone, even when they doubted themselves, was empowering. Witnessing the miraculous transformations and life-altering moments in the lives of my peers, I realized that my business was more than just a venture - it had become my mission field. However, I needed help figuring out how to channel this calling. And to be honest, that nagging fear of not being good enough haunted me like a persistent gremlin on my shoulder. I yearned to do more, to learn more, and to become more, but I felt lost in navigating this path in rebuilding parts of me while trying to excel more in my career.

Around 2012, our company introduced a new title to our career plan, igniting a fire within me and infusing my life with a newfound sense of purpose and motivation. This new role required me to develop twice as many leaders as before, which excited me as it was one of my favorite aspects of the business. I became hyper-focused and approached my career in a completely different way. It was exactly what I needed to continue on my journey of self-discovery during this season of my life.

2013 came and I proudly celebrated my promotion and embraced the latest addition to our career plan. With the collective efforts of other ambitious women seeking personal growth and leadership opportunities, we joined forces and charted a path toward a triumphant team victory. The feeling was indescribable. This new title marked a significant milestone in my career, and after nearly seven years, I genuinely realized that this was a transformative journey that profoundly shaped my purpose.

As I continued to excel in my new role, I began to see the impact of empowering others and helping them reach their full potential. It was a domino effect - as I lifted others, they, too, were motivated to do the same for those around them. This led to a positive shift in our team culture, where collaboration and support were at the forefront.

Through my direct-selling experience, I learned that true success is not just about achieving individual goals but also about lifting others and creating a culture of growth and development. This realization solidified my passion for leadership and personal growth.

I began actively seeking opportunities to mentor and coach others within my company and personal life. I also continued my journey of self-discovery and invested in personal development courses, certifications, and workshops.

Through these experiences, I discovered my true purpose - to empower others to reach their full potential and positively impact their own lives and the lives of those around them. This has become the driving force behind my career decisions as I strive to create a lasting legacy through empowering leadership.

Chapter 10

The Retreat

While I was proud to have earned this new title, I was also the youngest in that small elite group of top-level leaders, a distinction that came with its own challenges and opportunities. It was intimidating at times, diving into deep waters with vastly more experienced peers, but it also lit a fire within me to keep pace and realize the legacy my team was creating. While I slowly formed connections with some of the women in leadership alongside me, I truly bonded with only a few during our ascent to the top. Our lives were in different stages, and with the rapid growth we experienced, it often felt like a whirlwind. We found joy in our annual conferences and conference calls (before the age of Zoom), constantly cheering each other on. However, I never fully revealed my vulnerabilities to this group. The majority, including the company's leadership, remained unaware of the intricate details of my journey or the story that brought me here. I took great care in controlling the narrative and wanted to keep that the same.

As the number of individuals with this new title increased, we received an invitation to our inaugural top-level retreat. This retreat entailed spending an entire weekend at the owner's residence alongside our executive leadership and peers. Let

...ad confidence in my abilities when it came to ...s and the skills required to excel. I didn't mind ..., speaking, leading, coaching, or collaborating. How... this particular event filled me with nerves. It coincided ...ith another season of personal medical challenges, as I was grappling with neurological issues at the time. While a tinge of anxiety lingered, I relied on prayer, my husband, and therapy to navigate this familiar terrain. Vulnerability was already coursing through my veins.

Interestingly, my husband drove me to the retreat and remained close by, and it gave me an odd sense of comfort that I could call him to retrieve me at any time. It's a sad observation as I look back. As the weight of medical uncertainties loomed over us, I spent the six-hour drive attempting to empower myself with confidence and strength, assuring myself that I could attend this event and emerge unscathed. Notably, this group of women did not make me feel inadequate; congregating in a home environment instead of connecting remotely stirred my apprehension. This was our inaugural top-level event, and while excitement and pride coursed through me, there was also a tinge of fear.

The first few days of the retreat were a whirlwind of productive emotions and activities. We spent hours brainstorming, collaborating, and helping make critical decisions that would shape the future of our business. It was a bonding time; we shared laughter and tears, indulged in fine dining paired with exquisite wine, and celebrated our collective achievements. The environment was imbued with camaraderie and a celebration of our united endeavors.

The retreat transitioned into a new gear when a guest speaker, a professional in speaking and coaching, graced us with her presence. We'll call her Julie for the sake of this story. Her gift was to weave narratives that captivated and moved audiences, and she was there to help us knit our success stories into compelling tales for the next national conference. While confident in my professional skills, this was new territory. I'd often share a simplified version of what the business meant to me in the cozy quarters of living room parties, but this stage demanded more. My team knew of the themes of restoration and redemption that ran through my journey, yet I had never offered full disclosure. Now, faced with the prospect of baring my story on a grand stage, the challenge seemed daunting yet thrilling—a new chapter of vulnerability and connection waiting to unfold.

As I mulled over the task, I reassured myself that control was in my grasp—this was my narrative to shape. We divided into clusters, and the professional storyteller unveiled her expertise in these intimate gatherings. She illuminated the essence of a compelling narrative that captivates, engages, and resonates with the audience. Her coaching was meticulous—she guided us on inflection, gestures, and the subtle dance of narrating a tale. As she taught us the structure of breaking stories into three cohesive chapters, our group absorbed her wisdom like sponges.

We dispersed, seeking solitary corners of the house to translate introspection into words, our thoughts spilling onto paper. It was strangely cathartic, peeling back the layers of my professional journey, though a part of me yearned for the exercise's conclusion. That evening, nestled on a plush white sofa with a picturesque farm scene before me, I set my resolve. The rolling hills and distant cows served as a silent witness to my decision. My success story, ordinary yet authentic, would be segmented into three chapters, sprinkled with lessons learned and triumphs over trials. "Easy peasy," I whispered to myself, half believing it.

As we gathered once again, we were challenged to read our stories aloud to the group. With a makeshift microphone, we stood before everyone, sharing our tales. Julie, the master storyteller, guided us, pausing to ask thought-provoking questions, seeking the group's perspective, and pushing us to refine our tone and choice of words. We learned how to connect chapters and speak with confidence seamlessly. When my turn arrived, I steadied my hand and recounted my story from beginning to end. I deliberately paused to adjust my tone, transforming questions into assertive statements and choosing words to captivate and engage the audience. To be honest, it was an extraordinary experience that offered knowledge not easily acquired elsewhere. I appreciate her dedication and passion; storytelling is powerful and a key element of success in this particular industry. Stories can connect people, whether it's about a product or an opportunity. Thus, this experience proved to be invaluable. As I reached the climax and got closer to the finish line of my story, I locked eyes with Julie. With her arms folded and chin resting on one of her hands, her gaze softened, and she whispered, "It's a wonderful story. It might just be the one you tell yourself, or maybe it's just the one you tell your customers at your parties, but it's not the whole story."

My heart leaped into my throat, and I could feel the burning sensations of embarrassment spreading across my face and neck. I looked at her directly and mustered the courage to say, "This is the story you're getting," before taking a seat. What happened next is a blur; I only remember an awkward silence lingering momentarily. However, I do recall another leader stepping up and challenging her situation, shifting the mood in the room. Though no one was glaring at me, I couldn't help but feel all eyes were on me. I was disappointed and embarrassed and had to gather the strength to remind myself, "This story is more than fine. It's inspiring, comforting, and it brings a sense of joy." It's also the story I have told over and over again at my parties or opportunity events.

As the working session concluded, I rose from my seat and went to a nearby half-bathroom. Seeking a moment of solitude, I reassured myself that everything was alright. As I approached the edge of the carpet, ready to step into the hallway, a gentle hand slid up my back and settled upon my shoulder. I turned to find Julie standing there, leaning in and softly asking, "May I have a moment?" Without hesitation, I agreed, and together, we entered the front office of the house. Julie explained that this process was not about attacking or pressuring me to bear my life on paper. Instead, she posed a thought-provoking challenge, "If you had just one opportunity, a mere 10 minutes to stand on a stage and share your story with the world, one that would inspire and mark the headline of your legacy, would this be the story you would choose?"

In a soft, tearful whisper, I replied, "No." She explained that she saw something in me, a desire to control a narrative, to hide what lay beneath the surface. She reminded me that 99% of the room would be filled with women who had their own challenges and painful stories to share. This was my chance to inspire, to ignite belief, and to pave a new path for them. She asked me a thought-provoking question: If my daughter were in this situation, would I encourage her to embrace her true story or fabricate one for appearances bravely? Her words were gentle, spoken with affection. Whatever gave it away, she knew that my success in business and my discovery of a hidden version of myself were rooted in a story of redemption worthy of the stage. She offered me an assignment - instead of writing my story, I would journal my journey. It didn't have to be shared or used, but permitting myself to put the truth on paper would be a valuable step. From that experience, I could extract what felt comfortable and weave it into the chapters of my story. I agreed, feeling a sense of relief. This was something I could do. I had touched on it in therapy but never fully integrated it into a success story connected to my career, even though I knew they were intertwined.

While the rest of the group slept that night, I quietly slipped out of the dimly lit room filled with bunk beds. Seeking solace, I settled into a plush bean bag reminiscent of a sofa armed with a pen and notebook. Inspired by my therapy experiences, I began sketching circles on paper, carefully placing core memories and significant moments from my life within them. Connecting these circles with arrows and bullet points, I wove a tapestry of intertwined instances. As the clock approached 2 am, I transitioned from drawing to writing, skillfully crafting paragraphs that encapsulated my journey. Dividing my creation into three sections, I meticulously penned five pages that embodied the essence of my transformation from childhood to the present day.

Fatigue began to set in, but I felt relieved knowing I had conquered the challenge bestowed upon me. Deep down, I understood that this endeavor would remain unfinished had I waited until returning home. As the sounds of breakfast downstairs and the start of the morning shower routine filled the air, I realized I hadn't slept a wink. However, I reassured myself that I could catch up on rest during the journey back. Visibly, I was mentally drained and emotionally exposed, I recognized this project was not meant for the faint-hearted.

Nevertheless, I felt an immense sense of pride. I had embarked on a profound journey to extricate those thoughts from my mind, dislodge them from my heart, and finally transcribe them onto paper. This accomplishment marked a significant milestone in my personal growth and creative expression.

We packed up, had breakfast, and went downstairs for our morning sessions. However, I found it difficult to concentrate. Julie didn't join us that morning, but we were informed that we would continue our discussions through group calls and work on crafting our story for the upcoming convention. I felt a genuine connection with her, so I wasn't nervous but eager to complete this task.

Sitting among my peers, we reflected on the weekend and engaged in a group session. Towards the end, the floor was opened up for sharing. Typically, this involved discussing takeaways, moments of realization, or simply sharing general thoughts. If you've ever been part of these sessions, you know they can be pretty emotional. Taking women out of their everyday lives and permitting them to focus solely on themselves for a few days, reflecting on their successes, and setting goals for the future can be an incredibly transformative experience. Sometimes, the impact is overwhelmingly positive, while other times, it can be more challenging.

As individuals expressed their excitement for the future and shared what they had learned from the storytelling workshop, many were vulnerable enough to admit they were genuinely proud of themselves and our company. Meanwhile, my mind wandered, visualizing all the core memories I put on paper throughout the night. Although I was listening, the voice inside my head grew louder. I could feel a tingling sensation in my chest, and anxiety started to creep through my body, creating a warmth in my neck and a tingling in my nose. The room grew silent, and our fearless owner broke the silence, asking, "Anyone else?"

Regrettably, my mouth fell open without consideration, and words spilled uncontrollably. It's not about the time that has passed, as even 10 minutes later, I couldn't precisely recall what I said. However, I remember expressing the struggle of storytelling and sharing my journey through the dark seasons of life. Vulnerably, I acknowledged that the most important lesson I learned from this event was that stories don't have to be perfect. I hoped we could all gain something from this experience, understanding that our stories may not be pretty but uniquely ours. I also expressed deep concern that many of us likely have similar stories that we are too afraid to share and that our legacy has the potential to be greater than we ever imagined.

As I continued to speak, tears streamed down my face, completely unaware of the words pouring out of me. I concluded with the profound realization that, regardless of whether it made sense to anyone else, something truly profound had occurred to me that weekend. After nearly eight years in this industry, I knew I hadn't stumbled upon this opportunity by chance; instead, it had sought me out. It became an integral component of my healing journey, and I solemnly committed to navigating the depths of what that entailed.

I was overcome with emotion, unable to hold back tears. It was the kind of cry that leaves you breathless. The room fell silent as my colleagues glanced at me, and our company leaders occupied the corners. A close friend sitting near me discreetly took hold of my hand under the table. As the morning session drew close, gratitude was expressed for the rawness, progress, and personal growth we experienced over the weekend. I received numerous hugs, engaged in small talk, and received supportive acknowledgments. However, I departed that retreat a changed person from when I first arrived. I chuckled, realizing I nearly made it through without anyone suspecting I was anything but ordinary. Yet, deep down, I knew that the entire experience was far from ordinary. It was a pivotal moment in my life. That evening, on the car ride home, I sensed a shift taking place that would shape the course of my journey. It would lead me toward a path of restoration, storytelling, and making a lasting impact in ways I had never imagined possible.

Chapter 11

The Moment of Truth

I returned from the retreat with a profoundly renewed sense of purpose. In the coming month, I would channel my energy into transforming my story into a narrative I could share from the stage. The task seemed colossal: distilling 30 years of life experience into a concise, ten-minute presentation. With dedication, I began sorting through the significant chapters of my life, dividing them into three compelling segments for storytelling. My bathroom and car became sanctuaries for rehearsal, where I could read my drafts aloud and navigate the emotional undercurrents of my reflections. Sheets of paper were filled, crumpled, and rewritten, a cycle that captured the essence of diligence in my journey. As I progressed, a sense of pride swelled within me. This tangible representation of my experiences was a testament to my personal and professional growth. In a few months, I knew I would stand before an audience, unveiling facets of my success that had remained unspoken until now. The urgency of the effort was underscored by the looming date when I'd present my narrative to Julie for her review and input, a necessary step to ensure the accuracy and impact of my story.

On the day of my read-through with Julie, our company's founder and one of our leadership executives joined the call. With bravery, I began by expressing a deep and sincere gratitude for this opportunity. It was almost as impactful as years of therapy, and I am grateful that they showed a genuine interest in hearing our personal stories. They wanted us to deliver something other than some generic success story that could be replicated. Our company was more than just products and achievements. They wanted us to connect, to demonstrate that anyone can achieve success, regardless of their background. I read my story aloud, timing it to precisely 10 minutes, and proudly presented a narrative with a clear beginning, middle, and end. Now, let me clarify that it didn't include intricate details. Still, I transformed it into a captivating journey of pain, uncertainty, and disbelief, leading to self-discovery, restoration, healing, and a sense of purpose. Rather than the previous tale that showcased how I overcame medical debt, took a risk, and emerged on the other side triumphant. Amidst the conclusion of my story, a silence fell. Suddenly, Julie cleared her throat and spoke with conviction, "Don't change a single thing." It was a profoundly empowering moment as I sat in the parking lot of a restaurant, clutching my sheet of paper with an unshakeable smile. In that instant, a sense of liberation washed over me. Tears welled up in my eyes, but they were tears of release this time. I realized that my past no longer held sway over me. I longed for the moment and could finally take ownership of my journey. I no longer needed to fear the narrative. I could relinquish control and allow the truth to guide me.

Realizing I had an opportunity to impact thousands in this room, I nervously but delightfully embarked on dress shopping, planning my hairstyle, and practicing my story from start to finish. On a Friday night, in a ballroom filled with thousands of our consultants and their guests, I took the stage to deliver the story I'd worked so hard to craft. I was honest in sharing that a broken and abusive childhood had led me to become a young adult who was broken and unsure of herself, questioning her worth daily. While it wasn't an easy journey and full of challenging moments, I'd spent the better part of my career navigating a deeper purpose than just selling products and leading a team. I shared that this journey had unlocked my purpose and pursuit to impact other women and help their stories be told. To give them a voice. I proudly stood on that stage, took ownership of my story, claimed my voice, and committed to ensuring I was never silenced again. I would use this business as a mission field to reach other women.

I stepped off the side of the stage and spotted my colleagues and company staff radiating with pride. One person, in particular, was a longtime coach of mine at the company. He warmly embraced me, squeezing tightly. Another person cupped my cheeks, brimming with pride. As I made my way to my seat, I was greeted by my husband, sister, and mother, all standing and applauding with teary eyes. The moment of truth had arrived, and it felt incredible to stand there, knowing I had survived the stage moment and life itself. To be present in that very moment was so fulfilling. Later in the evening, as our awards night and fancy dinner drew close, I made my way from table to table, greeting my team, their spouses, and special guests. At each table, I was met with gratitude, pride, and, most importantly, their stories. I had promised these women that they could borrow my unwavering belief in them until they found their own, and I pledged to support them every step of the way. I was committed to helping them discover their voices; together, we would forge a path towards restoration. Stories can connect people, and when you are brave enough to share yours, it's truly remarkable what can unfold. By sharing our stories, we grant others a voice that may have previously remained unheard. It is a profound ability to unleash narratives that yearn to be told, waiting eagerly to break free.

Later that night, we returned to our hotel room. As I kicked off my heels, my husband's eyes met mine, and he uttered, "I'm incredibly proud of you." With a smile, I replied, "Me too." At that moment, I realized it was one of the first instances in my life where I genuinely felt a deep pride in myself. Not the kind of pride that comes from accomplishing something but the type that stems from genuinely embracing the person I have become. The anticipation of what the future held filled me with excitement and eagerness. I knew this was the beginning of my journey toward empowerment and helping others find their strength. And as I drifted off to sleep, I couldn't help but wonder what other amazing stories were waiting to be shared and heard. Because when we listen to each other's stories, we create a bond that transcends differences or barriers. We become united in our humanity, and that is a powerful force.

In the days following the event, I received numerous messages from attendees thanking me for creating a safe space for them to share their stories. Many expressed their desire to continue speaking their truths and helping others do the same. It was heartwarming to see how one act of vulnerability could spark a chain reaction of empowerment and connection. It reminded me that we all have the power to make a positive impact, no matter how small or insignificant it may seem.

Reflecting on my journey towards embracing vulnerability, I am grateful for the growth and strength it has brought into my life. It has allowed me to break free from societal expectations and live authentically. Still, most importantly, it has opened the door for me to connect with others on a deeper level and create meaningful change in the world.

My biggest hope is that I, along with others, continue to share our stories and listen to those of others. Let us embrace vulnerability and use it as a tool for empowerment and connection. Together, we can break down barriers and build a more compassionate and understanding society. Because our stories make us who we are and bring us closer to each other.

Chapter 12

The Unfolding Tapestry of My Legacy

The following year, I organized my team retreat at the same property where we had previously held our top-level event. Renting this location and hosting team gatherings became a special perk for upper-level leaders. The property was beautiful and provided a sense of security for me. Memories of being there still resonate with me, and although one might expect it to evoke negative emotions, it was at this very place that everything changed for me. There, I took ownership of my journey, embracing my story - the good, the bad, and the ugly.

Despite the hard work and exhaustion that came with these events, I absolutely loved organizing them. It was one of the most rewarding aspects of being a leader. Bringing together a group of diverse women, some of whom I barely knew due to our remote work arrangements before remote work became famous, was a truly enriching experience. We learned together and laughed together, and after long days of collaborative work, we would end the nights with laughter, dancing, games, and late-night conversations. Our ages ranged from 19 to 60, yet we formed a solid and cohesive unit, a family. I had hired my sister early in my career to assist me in running my business and managing these events. One of the greatest gifts this journey bestowed upon me was the ability to work alongside her. She played an integral role in my pursuit, challenging, supporting, cheering, and taking charge of the administrative tasks once I reached the top level and went full-time. It was only natural for her to join us at these events, and she had forged powerful bonds with many of my leaders. However, I decided to bring my mom along to lend a helping hand for this particular event. Hosting these events involved a lot of cooking, cleaning, setting up, and, not to mention, laundry.

As I glanced at the expectant faces before me, I took a deep breath and began our retreat unconventionally. Gone was the usual icebreaker. This time, my mission was clear: I wanted to set the tone, to peel back the layers of my own story as a testament to the transformative journey we were all part of. With my team's attention, I stood in the safe embrace of the home's lower level and revealed a more intimate picture of who I was beyond the titles and trophies. The projector sprang to life, casting images onto the wall, a visual timeline of a fractured and rebuilt life. From the remnants of my childhood to my turbulent teenage years and the serendipitous discovery of this opportunity, I shared the unfiltered truths. Over the next hour, my narrative unfolded—not just about the successes but how this work had cradled me in times of need, healed and honed my conviction, humbled and challenged my perspectives, and, ultimately, sculpted a pair of hands ready to serve a greater purpose. I was shaped by faith, and through this business, I found alignment with what I believed was my calling: to empower women to unearth their potential, ignite their passion, and journey toward a life of intention and fulfillment.

The rest of the night was a tapestry of vulnerability and strength, echoing through the room with a resounding depth that's difficult to articulate in mere words. Standing before these faces—my team, my community, my mother—I spoke of the abuse, a chapter of darkness I had never laid bare in such a way. In the raw openness of the evening, I witnessed something profound: a communal breath of catharsis. My mother, a pillar throughout my tale, silently absorbed every word, her presence a testament to resilience and a hope for healing. In turn, the room became a sanctuary where women, moved by this shared honesty, began to unravel their own tightly wound stories. Some voices reverberated with the strength of shared experience, while others whispered in the intimate corners of newfound safety. As discussions spilled into the early morning hours, the undeniable realization crystallized within me: my legacy would not be measured in quantifiable achievements but in the indelible marks of lives touched, paths redirected, and the silent victories of women who found the courage to rewrite their narratives, proving that the shadows of the past could indeed be eclipsed by a future crafted with purpose.

This home still holds a special place in my heart to this day. While my husband may think I'm joking, I often say that if I were to win the lottery (assuming I played), this would be one of the first doors I'd roll up to. A profound transformation took place within the walls of this house. It started with me, then extended to my team, and ultimately led to the birth of a mission and legacy. The redirection that occurred while being there sparked a chain of events that shaped our future.

The power of storytelling and vulnerability cannot be underestimated. It was through sharing my own story that others found the strength to share their own. This experience solidified my belief that our voices hold immense power, mainly when used to uplift and empower others.

In today's society, there is still a stigma surrounding discussions on abuse and trauma. Many people still shy away from these topics, fearing judgment or shame. But it is through open and honest conversations that we can break down these barriers and create a safe space for healing and growth.

As I continue my journey, I am constantly reminded of the impact of speaking our truths. It may not always be easy, but by sharing our stories, we heal ourselves and inspire and empower those around us. And with each person who finds the strength to speak their truth, the darkness of abuse is pushed back a little further, making way for light and hope.

I want women everywhere to know that they have the power to rewrite their stories, break free from the chains of past traumas, and create a brighter future for themselves and others. Maya Angelou once said, "There is no greater agony than bearing an untold story inside you." Let us speak our truths, break the silence, and build a world where everyone's stories are heard and valued. Our voices matter – they have the power to heal, inspire, and transform.

As my weekend retreat ended, a dear friend I met along this journey, Amy, approached me. She held my shoulders, ensuring I listened intently, and said, "I'll be the first in line to buy the book you'll write one day. Your story needs to be told."

While I had never entertained this idea, I considered it a gift. Though I appreciated the acknowledgment and support, I initially thought I needed more time and didn't need the world to know everything. However, I believe Amy had planted a seed because as the years went by, I continued to journal and document fragments of my life, mainly as a form of therapy. Yet, deep in my heart, a burning desire began to dream of a new path and a legacy that extended far beyond my immediate circle.

I wasn't sure how it would look, but I knew I wanted more for myself and a genuine connection with others. I discovered a talent for storytelling and building connections. While I enjoyed my work of selling products and building a team, my true passion lay in coaching, training, and mentoring others. It energized me and never felt like work. I often wondered how fortunate I was to get paid for doing what I loved. It was sometimes challenging, though. I faced challenges like a declining team, losing leaders, and financial setbacks. Working in a commission-based sales business was complex and emotionally demanding. However, my days were spent developing training, creating valuable content, nurturing leaders, providing support, and selling products I believed in. Despite the occasional gloom, it was far better than working a corporate 9-5 job, that's for sure.

Every party I attended had a new mission: to make an impact. We had fun, showcased products, and enjoyed good food, and I often stayed behind to help clean up and forge deeper connections with my hostesses. I gave back to my community as much as possible, supporting families during Christmas and donating to organizations and those in need. I knew that making an impact within the confines of a living room at a product party could extend beyond if I put in the effort. Sometimes, it was a financial gift; other times, it was a lending hand of volunteer work or an ear. This company, this circle of peers I had, made me want to be better. To do better. Being part of a community of supportive individuals who wanted the best for each other was something I cherished. I longed for genuine relationships, and while my immediate family was a robust support system, I embraced my new family that stretched beyond state lines, intertwining our lives and families. Some of my dearest friends were individuals with whom I had no team connection. Even spouses meeting on trips became lifelong buddies. I was proud to be a part of such a thriving community.

However, it's essential to acknowledge that not everyone gets along. When you bring a group of women together, there's bound to be some drama. Though these instances were rare, there were a few times when I was reminded that hurt people hurt people. One particular memory stands out: during a retreat in Destin, FL, our upper-level leaders gathered around the kitchen island one night and shared intimate details of our pasts. It was one of the first times I hinted at my childhood experiences before my breakthrough. We discussed the pain of feeling alone in our experiences, and one person bravely shared that a family member had abused her. Her courage inspired her siblings and cousins to follow suit. I barely had a chance to utter a few words, preparing to say, "That can be a lonely journey, and not knowing the outcome, it's scary to be the first to speak up." But before I could finish, another individual raised her hands and declared, "That's not trauma. What I went through was trauma."

My face contorted with wincing shock. I immediately turned to the lady beside me who had just shared her vulnerability, then directed my words to the individual who had just spoken and said firmly, "No one has the right, permission, or ability to decide what someone else's trauma is. Period."

The evening continued, and I eventually attributed the incident to some individuals having had too much wine. Nevertheless, I tried to seek out the leader who had opened up to us and provided support. I also was one of many who did that. In the following years, I consistently reached out to her, and she walked alongside me through my transformative healing journey. While I was furious with the person who spoke such harsh words, I must admit that the remark was etched into my memory and kept me silent for some time. Trauma cannot and should not be judged by others. It is a profoundly personal experience; remarks like that can hinder progress and pull someone further from healing.

Although I am far from perfect, I have always strived to show up as an authentic version of myself. The idea of hurting someone or causing them to doubt themselves is debilitating to me. However, growing up, I fit the definition of injured people. It's taken a lifetime of growth, maturity, and healing to stand where I am today. I dislike conflict and avoid drama, and I've learned the value of keeping my circle small.

In my home, we have a saying: "You can either react or respond to situations as they happen to you. Reaction stems from emotion, while response comes from consideration and reflection. You only get one shot, so choose wisely." I have been instilling this in my children since they were toddlers, and it serves as a daily reminder that I must embed deep within my soul.

As the years passed, I observed the individual who uttered those unkind words grow within the business. Through her own words, I learned that she, too, had her traumas to confront, and at that point, she had not faced them. This is the essence of my entire journey documented in this book: a cycle of pain, hurt, and turmoil that arises when we bury our feelings and obstacles. Eventually, they resurface, sometimes unknowingly, accidentally, sometimes under the influence of alcohol, and sometimes in moments of vulnerability. Regardless, I am constantly reminded that words have the power to impact someone else's life for an eternity. As women, we possess the ability to connect and uplift one another. We aim not to compete for success, titles, money, fashion, appearance, or material possessions. In reality, we are part of the same species; sometimes, no one understands us better than someone who has walked in our shoes. Unfortunately, we often fail to acknowledge this fact. Women are genuinely miraculous creatures; beautiful and unique things happen when we unite and link arms.

Chapter 13

Navigating White Waters

Please be advised that the narratives and reflections in this chapter are based on my personal experiences navigating professional challenges within my personal business and team. While the accounts are true to my perspective and recall, they may not universally represent the experiences of others involved or the industry at large. Different individuals may have varying recollections and interpretations of the events described. The intention is not to diminish or disregard the myriad challenges faced by all parties during these times, but rather to provide a personal viewpoint on the complexities encountered in the realm of business decision-making. This chapter aims to share insights from my particular path and is not a definitive guide for others. It is written in the spirit of learning and sharing and should be read as such.

Between the years of 2016-2018, our company faced challenges that marked a transformative phase of change and restructuring. Decisions that would lead to a significant adjustment within our compensation plan, triggering a range of emotions among our leaders. This became a turbulent stretch in the journey, and I felt completely overwhelmed and out of control. I reminded myself not to react out of emotion, to keep my blinders on, and not allow the many "I told you so" remarks to be louder than my own voice, knowing that skeptics were watching closely. Each day, I tried to encourage myself and my close peers. I had to choose whether to navigate the white water or fold over. It proved more difficult than I had anticipated, but I still felt purpose and opportunity there. I decided with my mind and heart that I was willing to ride the wave, regardless of the outcome. Like navigating rough waters, this chapter of my life demanded skills I had yet to develop fully, and it was one heck of a ride.

Our industry was already experiencing seismic shifts with the rise of social media prominence, the boom in online shopping, and waning interest in traditional living room parties. We were fiercely swimming through an unknown and uncharted territory. Until now, the company experienced explosive growth, catapulting us to become one of the fastest-growing party plan companies worldwide. However, growth often comes with growing pains, and over time—quite abruptly—it seemed our sales began to wane as customer acquisition and prospecting became more challenging than ever within my organization and many of my peers.

This period also coincided with the surge of new side hustles; the launch of the gig economy presented a fresh set of routes for many to explore. As the marketplace became more crowded, each product season we launched brought obstacles along with opportunities. Some you had to look for, while others smacked you in the face. It was a challenging season for many of us, but I am sharing my experience of this chapter of my journey with you because it was a pivotal moment in my career, and my response to it would alter the course of my life.

Oftentimes, when we read or hear about someone's success story, the difficult parts are either ignored or briefly mentioned. However, I believe that this particular chapter of my life has taught me several valuable lessons and helped me become the type of leader I always aspired to be. One who can face challenges and seize opportunities. As someone who works in this industry, I know that it can be like a roller coaster ride, requiring resilience and determination. My hope is that this chapter of my life will serve as an inspiration for those who may be experiencing a setback, a rut, or a life-altering change in their journey. It's important to remember that there is always life after the storm.

In full transparency, the changes implemented to stabilize our career plan and maintain compliance within the industry resulted in me losing the hard-earned title I had achieved and maintained for over five years. Notice I said resulting, not causing. While much personal growth and reflection brought me to that realization, I take responsibility for my own decisions that led to the decline of my business and organization.

It's wild how you can mourn a title, but being a goal-oriented person, it was one I was proud of. The loss of this title brought a significant shift in my compensation, resulting in a substantial decrease in income. This was undoubtedly a painful, incredibly emotional, and challenging experience. It felt like navigating through turbulent white water, waves crashing into me at each turn and some that seemed to appear overnight. Every single time I got my head above water, another wave hit.

Despite bracing myself for impact and tightening my life vest, I still believed that God had brought me this far for a reason and that this very large roadblock was not the end for me. I took the time to comprehend the changes and sought support from circles of women who propelled me forward rather than deterred me from my path. I even walked away from some relationships and social accounts that I felt were creating doubt and stirring fear within my fragile soul. I had to protect my state of mind and be intentional with the individuals I had conversations with or the circles I walked into. With determination, I focused my efforts and prayed with unprecedented fervor. Early in my business, I started it with prayer and many unknowns, handing it over to God from the get-go. Then, when I decided to pursue it even further and make it a career, I once again gave it to God. Not that I never stopped praying for direction and guidance and entrusting His hand in the entire process, but I feel I'd taken the front seat, and it was certainly a time to hand it back to Him.

Although that didn't remove the problems and obstacles that continued to arise, I remained steadfast in my belief in the opportunity. I had unwavering faith in the industry, my company, our mission, and our leadership. Despite the challenges, I trusted my decision in 2007 to enter this industry, and I now had to trust my decision to stay and rebuild. I challenged myself to step back and look at the bigger picture and I began to understand that some of the decisions and changes were necessary. Easy or fun? Nope. I also realized that I'd gotten quite comfortable in my leadership role, again not entrusting God's direction at all turns. I wasn't actively building the way I had all those years prior and wasn't leaning into prayer for decisions. I wasn't head-down-focused like I was all those years. I had never stopped working, but I can say I was working at a different pace that did not support healthy and sustainable attrition. My daily behaviors shifted over the years and I pulled myself away from some of the business behaviors that helped sustain my organization. Ultimately, with reflection, I took ownership that I was responsible for some of the decline in my own business. So when the compensation plan changed to require you to maintain the level of leadership you were sitting at and I was no longer maintaining it, it was simple. My organization no longer met the requirements of that title and so despite the pain of losing it, it was not mine to keep. It took a lot of reflection and growth, but I don't blame a single person or a single occurrence for the restructuring that took place. I look back and realize it was a journey of many challenges, and many of us had stopped rowing before the white waters even began. I take responsibility for the decisions I made along the way, realizing much later on that getting comfortable in a position, title, or income opportunity can come with consequences. Don't get so comfortable you stop rowing. You can coast, you can balance between play and work and enjoy the scenery, but you coast with the plan to pick up the oar and keep rowing.

I just wasn't prepared for the aftermath, which would force me to decide whether to rebuild or haul tail—mentally, physically, emotionally, or financially. Sometimes, I had to decide on it every morning when I got up. Call me crazy or naive, but I decided to stick around, rebuild, regrow, and trust the journey. I just knew deep down that I was meant to be here and stay here. I had a decided heart; I was sticking to it.

They say there are stages of grief in any loss, regardless of its nature, and I found myself grappling with a whirlwind of emotions as I progressed through each stage and truly grieved the loss of my title, my income, and a good chunk of my organization. There were moments when I felt motionless, carefully concealing my depression and fear that was nearly paralyzing at times. I couldn't sleep, I couldn't eat, I couldn't enjoy moments. I was far from present, and I battled a distressing journey of losing control. I was still aware that a decision had been made, and I was choosing to stay, which meant grabbing an oar or jumping ship. My business wouldn't rebuild itself. No one else would do the work for me, and it wasn't my job to convince anyone to stay or go; this was about me and my decision to put one foot in front of the other.

Over the following years, I witnessed several of my peers make their own decisions, and many decided to leave. Some embarked on new journeys elsewhere, while others bid farewell to the industry entirely and focused on finding their own path. Some went back to corporate; some stepped into a calling of ministry or industry coaching. Meanwhile, I worked diligently to remain focused on strengthening and stabilizing my organization and leadership team. It was painful to see a lot of the people I had worked so closely with leave, and it can mess with your emotions as you navigate the storm. Did I do the right thing by staying? I'd been offered several opportunities to leave and go to other companies, some even willing to bring me over at the same title and replace my lost income. On the surface, it seemed like the thing to do. However, the idea of walking away from my team and what I'd built, leaving the mission I so strongly believed in, seemed suffocating to even think about. It caused a physical ache.

Did I have some meltdowns? Yes. Did I wallow in self-pity at times? Yes. Did I ever consider just walking away from it all? Of course. I had to remind myself daily what the ultimate goal was, that my vision was still alive, and I had to unlock a fight in me I hadn't tapped into for a long time. I wasn't sure she was still in there, but with some digging...I did find her. Through reading books, leaning into my mentors and my safe circles, praying, and surrendering, I began to see the water settle around some turns.

With a desire to rebuild and determination that I had to dig deep for, I began to patch the holes in our figurative boat, taking each day as it came, supporting my team, and devising plans. Strategically exploring innovative approaches to attract new customers, I overcame the doubts that washed over me like waves in tumultuous waters while rebuilding faith in our industry, brand, and the opportunities ahead. Some days were challenging, and on those days, I wanted to point fingers or blame others for where I'd ended up. I grappled with understanding why the ship had taken this particular course at times, especially considering all the positive aspects and comparing past seasons to this one I was in.

Furthermore, numerous naysayers emerged from the shadows, insisting it was time to abandon the business as if the train had stopped. Amidst the chorus of doubters exclaiming, "You don't own that business; you have no control! I told you so!!!" I stood firm. I held onto my business with white knuckles and guided my team forward. For those who wanted to stay and ride the waves with me, we held onto each other and trusted the path ahead.

Every day, corporate leaders face the weight of decisions shaping their companies' trajectory, vitality, and prosperity. I understood the gravity of these choices, even when it came to my own business and team. Though challenges arose, the company persisted, an opportunity remained available, and we shifted our focus to fortify its present well-being and position it for long-term growth.

I was resolute in my decision. I had a decided heart. I had endured challenging seasons, relying on prayer and entrusting this business to God long ago. I had to tap back into that mindset and shift from control to needing to be led. My dedication to the mission remained at the forefront of my heart, and there was still work I desired to accomplish here. I could spend endless hours playing the blame game, seeking refuge in avoidance, or wallowing in loss. I had to stop looking behind me. Instead, I chose to gather my strength, making difficult decisions for my family's financial well-being. Eventually, with renewed determination, I fastened my seatbelt and prepared to navigate the uncertain future, believing the white water was nearly behind me.

Just about the time I felt like the water was calming...

A phone call would remind me again that I am not in control.

Chapter 14

Hey Girl

Although my biological father's family still resided nearby, our once strong connection was severed due to the tumultuous relationship with my father. Throughout my life, I occasionally encountered cousins, aunts, and uncles, who always greeted me with kind words and warm hugs. Some even expressed their pride in me and often apologized for my father's absence on his behalf, mostly my uncles. Over the years, there were moments when my father reappeared in my life, frequently coinciding with important milestones. For example, when he heard about the birth of my daughter, he called my sister to inquire about my well-being, or the time I ran into him at a grocery store, shopping for my daughter's birthday, and invited him to come. He only met my children a few times at certain events, so I waited to reveal his true identity to them until they were older. Considering he had moved away and was building his own life, I didn't need to make the situation messy for my kids to understand. I was very protective of that.

Each time he reentered my life, he professed a desire to repair our relationship. His famous words were, "I want to do better, and I'll call you next week." Every single time, I desperately hoped that things would be different, but he would inevitably return home, leaving me waiting another year to hear from him. Let me clarify that I am well aware that a relationship takes effort from both sides, and I did attempt reconciliation several times. However, I wouldn't say I liked having to beg for his attention. Especially as an adult, I was so tired of asking for him to want to know me, see or spend time with my family. He missed significant milestones in my life, remaining unaware of who his grandchildren were and missing out on the lives my sister and I had created. He remained oblivious to our professional lives, unaware of the battles we had endured without his knowledge or support. He never inquired about my childhood or checked in on me. He consciously chose to live a life without my sister and me, and as I grew older, this became increasingly difficult for me to comprehend as a parent myself. I had forgiven him long before most would, but the idea of rebuilding our relationship became more distant and seemingly impossible, and I eventually gave up.

The day that the phone call came was on a Sunday evening while we were visiting Ryan's grandparents. It was my uncle, my father's brother. I was taken aback to hear his voice on the other end. He informed me that my grandfather was sick, battling Leukemia, and his condition was quite serious. After further discussion, it was clear that my uncle was incredibly emotional, sharing his frustration that the physicians were mishandling his medical care and diagnosis. I could hear the fear in his voice. Without hesitation, I found myself in their living room within 24 hours. This wasn't easy for me, and I was incredibly nervous, but as I entered, that emotion left. My Grandpa immediately acknowledged me with a smile and gave me a "Hey, Girl." He was such a light-hearted spirit, full of jokes, and excellent at putting others at ease. Despite looking quite pale, frail, and tired, he still made me smile within seconds. His voice provided a strange sense of comfort to me that day.

A home health nurse was present, monitoring his vital signs. She looked at my uncle and said, "He needs to go to the hospital." Suddenly, the evening turned into an unexpected overnight stay in the hospital, surrounded by family members whom I hadn't seen in over a decade. Despite the passage of time, my love for my grandparents remained unwavering. I always wondered if they truly knew the depth of my pain and feeling of betrayal, and in that moment, I deeply regretted not being there for them all those years. I regretted that I hadn't allowed my children to know them. I must admit I had no valid excuses for my absence other than that I didn't believe I could maintain those relationships; mentally, I never felt strong enough to attempt it. I didn't think they were conducive to my healing and recovery process. During my visits in my teenage years and early twenties, something always seemed to go wrong. My grandparents were always good to me, but it was a persistent battle for others to understand what had happened between my father and me; I felt it was up to him to mend that and explain to his family what had happened all those years prior. Eventually, it was just easier not to deal with any of it.

Sitting in the emergency room waiting area, I was overwhelmed by the realization that I was suddenly here. I remember looking around and the surreal feeling that I was sitting amongst this side of my family. My beloved uncle, who cared for my grandparents daily while raising his granddaughter, came out and beckoned me to join them in the room. He asked me to stay and consult with the doctors so that we could fully understand the prognosis and treatment plan. As a single father who had undoubtedly carried the weight of responsibility for most of his life, he appeared visibly exhausted. He had huge bags under his eyes and looked overwhelmed and almost defeated. His daughter had drained him emotionally, and he had always been the one to take care of my grandparents' home, finances, and health. I could only imagine how he felt sitting there in this room. I glanced at him while my grandfather rested, and my heart hurt for him. I knew they had never faced a prognosis like this before, nor had they anticipated the possibility of numerous medical visits and decisions. I remember the sadness that overwhelmed me as I realized that he was carrying loads of burdens.

As the doctor approached, I sat in the corner in a cold, black, uncomfortable chair. The room was bright, large, and freezing. The room had such a somber heaviness that it made my chest heavy. I could feel anxiety rising as I swallowed, took a deep breath, and pressed my lips together, trying to gather myself. The doctor asked about the chemotherapy plan, and I glanced at my uncle. He replied, "Well, here's the thing... we just found out about this." The doctor argued, "No, he was diagnosed three months ago, and he was supposed to start chemotherapy the following week."

After an emotional conversation, I realized that a precise diagnosis had not been effectively communicated. My grandmother had been informed during a follow-up appointment. Still, she failed to comprehend fully, and the overseeing physician neglected to arrange the cancer treatment, resulting in no follow-up from our family or even the facility. I wasn't there, and I don't know the conversations that took place, but it is evident that this was news to my family that week. It sounds unbelievable. Like, how does this even happen?

My uncle and I visited the administrator's office the following day and received apologies, but they admitted that someone had dropped the ball. My grandfather had been diagnosed with Leukemia and sent home, only to rapidly decline three months later, not fully being aware of what was happening. I wanted to sit there and go to battle, but realizing this was not the time, as his care was a priority, and we needed answers. I was floored that even the home health nurse who came to assess his heart did not know his diagnosis. The entire situation felt like a bad movie. I was terrified of all the unknowns and questioned how in the world this even happened.

The night before, as we began to receive the news and discuss a care plan, I called my sister and biological father to explain, and soon, my sister came over while my father began his journey back to Virginia. Thanks to my career choice, I was blessed with a flexible schedule and devoted my days and nights to being by my grandfather's side as often as possible. Over a couple of weeks, we would all alternate nights and days with him. To my delight, no one ever made me feel like an outsider. Nearly 20 years had passed, yet there were no questions or concerns about our lost time. We shared stories, laughter, and cherished precious moments with my Grandpa. Eventually, he was discharged and finally stable enough to begin his treatments. I accompanied him to several sessions, where we would laugh, chat, and reminisce. He was a favorite in the cancer center, often winking at me that the ladies couldn't resist an older man in need. Despite the heaviness in those centers, I developed a new fondness and compassion for those nurses. There was one in particular who was a family friend, and the love she showed him was something I'll forever cherish. She took the time to explain things to me, often just holding me in an embrace that told me I needed to remain strong but to cherish the moments.

The treatments took a toll on him, leaving him drained. Just after 2-3 sessions, he had a near-fatal episode at home, and we had to call an ambulance. As they wheeled him out of the front door, I leaned over the shoulder of the EMS team, and we all assured him, "We'll be right behind you."

He said out loud for all of us to hear, "I won't be coming back home."

We arrived at the hospital and discovered that he required a blood infusion and would most likely need one after each treatment. So, we settled into a hospital room with a view of the busy city and did our best to make him comfortable. He was exhausted, in pain, and lacking the energy to fight most days. In between those moments were his wisecrack jokes and contagious laugh.

Although there were a few moments of unfamiliarity when it was just the two of us, he would always lighten the mood with his humor, effortlessly breaking the tension. When he wasn't asleep, we repeatedly watched Andy Griffith and talked about how gross the hospital food was. I could tell he struggled to accept my help, but he would often request that I stay longer or be the one to stay on certain nights. I would sit in the side chair, the soft glow of my laptop illuminating the room, grateful for the flexibility to work from anywhere. I would wash his hair, bathe, assist him in using the bathroom, and shave his face. The younger version of myself had no idea how much I would treasure those moments, but I soon found solace in that hospital room. One night, as the room lay in darkness, with only the faint glow of streetlights seeping in, he broke the silence and said, "Hey, girl." I leaned in, eager to help him; I assumed to use the bathroom. Instead, he wanted to talk.

I have only shared this entire conversation with one person, but considering its profound impact on my life, I feel compelled to put it on paper and honor the moment, as it brought me immense healing I didn't know I needed. He said, "Scoot over here."

I grabbed his hand and dragged the heavy reclining chair to his bedside. He turned his head towards the window, and the streetlights created a soft glow on his face. I just stared at him. I had a moment of realization, wondering how many memories I'd lost due to our restraint, and I suddenly became jealous of my cousins who had been there the entire time. I felt immense guilt suddenly, and it ached. Until the crack of his voice broke my thoughts, he said, "I'm ready to go home. I'm ready to go to Heaven." Chills covered my arms and prickled the back of my neck, and as tears escaped me, I said, "Is your heart ready?" He smiled and said, "Yeah, I'm sure." This man had been in church his entire life, a master at playing the dobro and making beautiful gospel bluegrass, so it felt like a silly question, but when you are faced with a conversation like this and have an opportunity to ask, you make sure of it.

He continued, "Someone will need to take care of grandma. She ain't well." Confused, thinking maybe he meant after she lost him, he broke my train of thought and continued. "She's confused and needs someone to stay with her." I could tell he didn't have the strength to get into conversation, so I just chose to listen, contemplating what that truly meant. But what happened next broke the stillness of the room as uncontrollable sobs left my body. He met my eyes and said, "I'm sorry your dad left ya'll. We've lost a lot of time."

The pain that I had been suppressing overwhelmed me as I lowered myself and rested my tear-streaked face on his hand. With gratitude, I managed to whisper, "Thank you, Grandpa." He allowed me to stay there, crying. That night, profound healing washed over me, reconnecting the fragmented pieces of my heart. Rising to meet his gaze, I noticed his closed eyes. Gently, I stood up, kissed his forehead, and murmured, "I love you, and I'm so sorry I haven't been here." Settling back into the recliner, which I left beside him, we drifted off to sleep together, still holding hands.

I had never shared that story with anyone except my husband. It held immense significance to me, and as I reflect on it now, I realize that if my uncle hadn't called and I hadn't mustered the courage to show up despite my fears of rejection, I wouldn't have had the privilege of those precious weeks with him. Each moment was treasured, every laughter absorbed.

Eventually, he was transferred to the ICU. On the last day that my grandfather was still lucid, my cousin and I took the initiative to bathe and shave him so he could see Grandma. We carefully washed his head, cleansed his body, and shaved his sunken face. Remarkably, he cracked jokes, laughed, and displayed a surge of energy that had been absent for a while. He was like a completely different person. I'd seen something they call "the surge" in TV shows, and I did my best to push that thought out of my mind. I wanted to be present, and hearing his laughs and jokes gave me hope. Just as my cousin left the room to bring Grandma in for a visit, he maintained a forward gaze, avoided eye contact with me, and uttered, "Hey. Don't you let them keep me in here, k?" Before I could even respond, Grandma entered the room. I discreetly stepped out and exited the ICU, overwhelmed by a mixture of fear and anxiety that made my face tingle and my cheeks flush. Confused at first, I suddenly understood his intentions. He knew his children would do everything in their power to keep him alive, but he did not desire that outcome. Yet somehow, I was holding onto the knowledge of his wishes, and it felt so uncomfortable.

I later learned that a doctor had already spoken to him and informed him they would meet with the family. My father, uncles, and aunts gathered in the waiting room and motioned for me to join them. The doctor explained that his condition was deteriorating, and despite having a good day, a decision was needed regarding his care. My family began to argue about how good he felt that day, and deep down inside, I knew what the sense of energy was that day. The doctor explained that he would either continue with treatments, which would require infusions until he could no longer withstand the sickness and discomfort, experiencing excruciating pain each time, or we could stop the treatments and focus on making him as comfortable as possible for his remaining days in the hospital. I spoke up and asked about the prognosis if we chose to continue treatments, to which the doctor replied, "Maybe a few months." Sitting a few chairs away from me, my father asked, "What would those months look like?" Without hesitation, the doctor responded that he would eventually become incoherent as they would need to administer pain medication to manage the treatments and infusions.

As I opened my mouth and my words broke in waves, I mustered the courage to speak up and locked eyes with my uncle. "He doesn't want that," I said. "He wants us to let him go." To my left, my aunts broke down in uncontrollable sobs. Deep down, I knew it wasn't fair. It wasn't easy to express. But just an hour ago, the man had confided in me about his wishes. It wasn't my decision; I wasn't even a regular part of his everyday life. Yet, I felt a profound obligation to be truthful because I knew my Grandpa trusted me implicitly. In that solemn moment, they handed my uncle a clipboard, along with a pen and a piece of paper. He stared at it intently, contemplating the weight of the decision. Eventually, he signed it and passed it along. As a family, we recognized that this was the turning point, and now it fell upon someone to break the news to my grandma and hope she could fully understand that there wasn't another option.

A few days later, he was transferred from the ICU to the top floor of the hospital. Unbeknownst to me, this floor turned out to be the farewell floor. As I arrived for a visit, a sense of unease washed over me, permeating the room. The hallways were empty; the floor was completely silent. Although I was young when my nanny passed away, I vividly remember the visits, her hospital room, and the bittersweet moments of saying goodbye. However, this time felt downright terrifying, and I was well aware of the lingering heaviness in their air.

My sister and I made regular visits during those days, crossing paths with our cousins and getting used to the everyday presence of our father, who had taken time off from work to be here and stay in Virginia. We took over the waiting room often, filling the air with laughter and sharing stories. It was as if time stood still, and for brief moments, I was transported back to my childhood. Despite the sad circumstances, my father embraced his role as a jokester, entertaining us with hilarious stories, reminiscing about Grandpa, and recounting his cherished childhood memories.

A layer of melancholy lingered over us as we settled in to stay one night at the hospital together. I lay across from my father in a row of waiting room chairs as we laughed together and tried to get sleep. However, I distinctly remember closing my eyes that night, feeling a glimmer of hope. This may be the turning point for our family. Maybe Grandpa was bringing us back together.

Two days before he passed away, my sister and I found ourselves alone with our grandma in the hospital room on the top floor. Knowing we would be there, my uncle brought her for a visit and dropped her off. Truthfully, up until now, this entire time, I hadn't spent a lot of time with her. She seemed feeble, strangely quiet, and overwhelmed by the situation, so my uncle only brought her for daily visits. She sat quietly, holding a newspaper and a raincoat, her hands resting in her lap. Suddenly, she stood up and declared, "Well, it's time for me to go."

I sprang up, knowing she couldn't leave alone, hoping she understood that too. Throughout this ordeal, she had rarely been displaying normal behavior. To me, anyway, and I had to remind myself I hadn't been around her in years. I honestly assumed her unusual demeanor resulted from the situation. I had even asked a few people about her, but my concerns were brushed off. After my Grandpa's remark, I began worrying that more was beneath the surface. Approaching her, I reassured her that my uncle would return soon to take her and that, in the meantime, we would stay together. Grandpa was unconscious due to the medication, so it was just my sister and I attempting to engage in conversation with her. She grew frustrated and belligerent, storming into the hallway, insisting she was going upstairs to prepare dinner before Grandpa got back from fishing. Like a crashing wave against the shore, I was overwhelmed by the realization that my grandma was unaware of what was happening. It actually horrified me at that moment. Initially, I attributed it to the stress of the situation, but I hadn't been around this woman for over 15 years, and I wasn't sure about the extent of our predicament. My emotions heightened, as I had no clue how to handle this situation, and my sister's shocked face flashed by me as my grandmother continued to yell in my face, insisting she was leaving. A nurse hurried down the hallway, and in sheer fear and confusion, I turned to my sister, attempting to comprehend it all. I shared with her what Grandpa had said, and together, we concluded that perhaps she had dementia, and maybe this situation was exacerbating it.

We called my uncle, and then I informed him and my dad about the situation, explaining what Grandpa had shared with me. It was clear to all of us that he had been looking out for her for a while, as the memory loss and confusion would come and go. I'm convinced the situation only added to the confusion and took her to a place she couldn't return from.

In his final days, my sister and I visited Grandpa, sitting in the room with my uncle and our father. The atmosphere was heavy, but it sparked a conversation about why Grandpa was holding on. Once full of vitality, his frail body had grown even more pale and weak. I prayed silently, hoping he couldn't feel any pain. Unsure of what he was hanging on to.

Usually, we would share stories and have small talk amongst him lying there, but something shifted that evening. I locked eyes with my father and spoke urgently as a thought had come to me. "You have to let him go. Assure him you'll care for Grandma and promise we'll be alright without him." He stared at me, tears welling up in his eyes. Slowly, he rose and leaned close to my Grandpa's ear. Through trembling words and a voice overcome with emotion, my father did just that. We would spend the next 30 minutes taking turns bidding our final farewells, whispering messages to departed loved ones he could pass along, and reassuring Grandpa that Grandma would be taken care of. It was heartbreaking, and it absolutely destroyed me to watch two grown men say goodbye to their dad.

In the midst of it all, my father, sister, and I wrestled with a multitude of emotions. The past few months had been a whirlwind, but we hadn't indeed acknowledged the weight and uncertainty that hung over us. It was as if we silently vowed to leave the past behind for now. That night, my heart shattered for my father. Navigating my emotions became arduous, and my sister and I were left pondering the unknown future, all while grappling with the intermittent loss of our Grandpa. Yet, amidst the pain, things felt somewhat hopeful. The journey through the white waters of my life had been remarkably relentless. But this was a new body of water. Over those two years, I had faced one obstacle after another in my career, only to be confronted with the haunting presence of my past and a tidal wave of emotions, family dynamics, and heartache. It was a lot to take in as we left the hospital that night, pretty much praying Grandpa through the gates of Heaven.

The following day, Grandpa met Jesus.

Chapter 15

Choose Me

At the age of 14 and beyond, it was like playing a game of Red Rover with my biological father. I never knew when he'd want me around, and I hated having to be the one who asked. A lot had changed between us, but I still loved him. I wanted a relationship with him, but the relationship and the desire for one faded over time. After everything that had happened with my stepdad, the distance grew, and the unspoken pain nestled comfortably in between us. Calls became less frequent, visits became more distant, and sometimes a year would go by without contact. I did visit several times when I first got my license at 16, but there was another long gap following that. It wasn't until I got engaged at 19 that conversations started again when I called to share the news of this milestone. Whatever little connection we had left entirely went up in flames the night of my bridal shower, just months after my engagement. After that, we'd have a conversation maybe every 2-4 years. Every time I saw him, I would try to gather the courage to have a difficult discussion and ask him, "Don't you ever wonder about me? About us? About my sister? Our kids?" I always chickened out, as much as I wanted to know the answer...I didn't want to know the answer. As I became a parent, I just struggled so deeply to understand and comprehend how someone could choose not to be part of their children's lives or how they could have grandchildren they knew nothing about.

No matter how brave I felt or how far I'd convinced myself I'd moved on, all the walls would come tumbling down when I saw him. It's like I would spend all that time building it while we were apart, and as soon as I heard from him or saw him, the little girl in me longed for him, and my hopes would skyrocket once more. It was so frustrating, and I was always mad at myself.

I had gone for years without talking to him, except for the occasional birthday text, until my grandfather fell ill. So, immersing myself in that life wasn't the most comfortable thing, but looking back, I didn't give myself a chance to decide otherwise. It wasn't the time or place to decide that. That night in the emergency room, finding out he had cancer and hadn't started treatment was too much for me to walk away from. That night, I made up my mind; I wasn't going anywhere, no matter how uncomfortable it got.

If there's one thing I've always known about my father is that he's not a fan of confrontation. Instead, he's a pro at sweeping things under the rug. In his world, we pretend that nothing has ever happened, like no time has ever been lost. So, I knew it would be up to me to put all my feelings aside and just be present. This wasn't the time or place to hash this out. Every day, he would come in and sit with me in the waiting room, and we'd talk about Grandpa, sharing memories of the good times they had together. I would listen, reminiscing about my own cherished moments over the years. We never really talked about "us". We never discussed the years he missed, or that I had a whole life, he knew nothing about. He asked a few questions about my job, husband, and the kids, but he had no clue who I was. Not really. And yet, here we were - sharing the same blood, going years without seeing or talking to each other, and thrown into an uncomfortable and sad situation that landed us in a waiting room together.

Despite the challenges of Grandpa's illness and passing, at times, I started enjoying my time with him and couldn't help but wonder how things would've been if nothing had changed. One evening in the hospital waiting room, it was just us. He had just finished a phone call with my stepmom and returned to the room, plopping down next to me and sighing. I glanced at him and asked if everything was alright. He shrugged and said, "She's wondering when I can return home since I've missed so much work."

I had to bite my tongue. I chose to say nothing.

He went on to say, "Being here is so different. I feel happier here. It's sad, though, knowing that my dad is dying in another room. But I've enjoyed being here with you, Hope."

I swallowed the lump in my throat and moistened my lips. Tears welled in my eyes as I leaned against his shoulder and said, "Yeah, it does. You seem like your old self." We locked eyes and shared a few moments of silence until he finally spoke. With a sincere expression, he said, "Things will be different. They have to be. I need to take control of my life and do better."

I replied by promising to do the same and reminding him that he couldn't just go home and do his usual thing...forget about me. We kept chatting a bit, and he opened up about some of his life, things I'd never heard before that got me thinking that this time felt different. Like he was suddenly realizing how quickly time flies and how much he's missed out on, and he knew he had to make some tough choices.

This particular conversation was just between the two of us, and it left me really emotional. I called my mom on the way home from the hospital that evening and told her everything that had happened, tears streaming down my face. Even though we were going through this significant loss, I felt a glimmer of hope that I hadn't felt in a while. I tried to hold back my excitement because I didn't want to get my hopes up too high. But deep down, I couldn't help but think that maybe Grandpa had indeed brought us all back together. I remember driving home that night, imagining how great it would be for him to spend time with my kids and for me to share my accomplishments and life with him. Just a few days after this conversation, my Grandpa passed, and my mom went to pay her respects and stop by their house. She later told me she had a heart-to-heart with my father outside the front door. She said she expressed how much this time meant to me and hoped he wouldn't fall back into old patterns when he got home. She wanted him to mean it when he said he would make an effort, no matter what. I'm not sure exactly how he responded, but I do know he expressed his own appreciation for our time and understood that he needed to make this time different.

Days later, we started planning the funeral. I went to the funeral home with the family and helped choose a casket and make service decisions. It was tough, as I had never done this for anyone before. My father was falling apart during this time, and I was grateful to be there with him and his family. We cried, we laughed, we remembered, and we made decisions that nobody likes to make. There were a couple of days until the funeral, and honestly, I wasn't sure if my father drove back home to get my stepmom and siblings or if they drove in. I hadn't seen him in a few days, but we had been texting back and forth. As I got out of the car in the parking lot of the funeral home, I saw my father standing near the curb. My husband and kids followed behind me, and he met me in the middle of the parking lot. I hugged him, feeling the stiffness of his suit as I embraced him. Stepping back, I made eye contact with him, and we exchanged a few words, nothing in particular until I noticed a sudden change in his demeanor. His shoulders drooped, his eyes fell, and I could hear my husband shuffling his feet uncomfortably behind me as my father broke eye contact with me. I looked around and saw my stepmother walking towards us across the parking lot without saying a word to me. She placed her hand on my father's shoulder and said, "We better get inside."

It's been more than ten years since I last saw this woman. But as she walked by me, my husband, and my two kids, my cheeks turned red, and I instantly knew. It was like a knife in my stomach, and I physically remember touching my stomach and swallowing slowly. Taking a deep breath, I realized it at that very moment.

Nothing would change.

I never really get what happens when he leaves and goes back home. Or how his mood shifts when he receives a phone call while he's with me. We never really talk about it, and even though I have a million questions, I decided not to dig any further a long time ago. Walking into the funeral home with my family, bringing my kids to meet blood relatives they've never seen and say goodbye to a grandfather they didn't know, I spent the evening watching everyone mourn my bluegrass pickin' Grandpa who loved the Lord, loved to fish, and loved this family. I did my best to hold myself together, but I couldn't help but mourn all the time lost, and it came down to the fact that none of us were willing to have hard conversations over all these years. It wasn't one person's fault. I wasn't a victim. At the end of the day, it comes down to everyone being willing to say the hard things, but with this family, that doesn't happen. No one will admit any wrong; no one says, "I'm sorry," for as long as I can remember, my sister and I were always made out to be the ones at fault for walking away. Walking away and creating boundaries are very different from each other. While I wasn't the best at maintaining them when it came to this, I intentionally made those boundaries to try and protect myself and the life I wanted to build. Being here, in this funeral home with all of these people, made me hyper-aware of why I'd done that so many years ago, and I swallowed the emotion down the entire evening, trying to wrap my head around all that had happened in just a few months.

My stepmom only said "Hi" to me that night. She never met my kids; truthfully, I didn't care for her too. In full transparency, we never had a good relationship once she started having her own kids. Her relationship with my sister and I changed once she became a mom. However, I never mourned that because, in all honesty, I've never desired one with her. I'm not afraid to admit that, and I won't pretend I haven't felt that way all these years. I knew how she felt about me, which made me want to protect myself. I'm not innocent in the situation; I'm sure my actions and words have made it clear that I don't want things to change between us over the years. However, once you realize you can't trust someone and they can manipulate people and situations in their favor, I knew having a bond would never happen. I forgave a long time ago, but forget? Not when it's repetitive behavior. Unfortunately, I can't think of a single thing I did to make things turn out this way. It just happened over time.

That said, I was just a kid when she came into my life. I was a kid who needed parents to step up, but instead, with distance, name-calling, and accusations, I closed my heart off from trusting any words that were said. The night of my bridal shower showed me how she felt about me. When I called my dad to ask why he didn't come, I was crying and also yelling, and he could barely get a word in. They had accused me of lying about a pregnancy. Apparently, someone had told them I was hiding it, which was my reason for an urgent marriage. It's not like I could hide that; I kept screaming back to him.

I kept asking, "Why wouldn't you just ask me? Instead, accuse me of lying and missing out on an important event in my life?!"

Amid my yelling, my stepmom grabbed the phone from my father and said, "Listen here, you little b****."

I couldn't believe it. My jaw dropped, and I looked at Ryan, who immediately made a turn and parked the car on a side road. I had them on speakerphone. His face showed pure shock, and my heart sank into my stomach. My mind was racing, but I couldn't process any thoughts. She had never spoken to me like that, and at that moment, her tone and words told me everything about how she felt about me. It infuriated me, but it also broke my heart, and in all honesty, I knew then that she and I would never be able to mend anything between us.

The little bits of what remained of my father and me after that night were like shards of glass I continued to pick up and try to put back together over and over again. Looking back, I was scrambling to find pieces I could use. I yearned for it, and despite having a dad who wanted to be in my life, that desire to look for pieces to repair what was broken never truly went away. There's a painful churn in your heart when you feel like a parent doesn't choose you. You grow up wondering why a parent can love another child like they should have loved you. I love my half-siblings, and sometimes I wonder what their life was like, but I'm also painfully aware he was there and present for them.

Since that fiasco, there's never been a sincere apology. And now here we were again, faced with one another amidst the loss of my Grandpa. Would anything change between my father and me?

It happened just as I expected it would.

Almost a year passed since Grandpa had died, and we hung out a few times and texted every few months. It wasn't exactly what I wanted, but I saw it coming. I was so mad at myself for opening that door again and frustrated that I couldn't get my act together and move on. I could have told him when my Grandpa was sick about the boundary I'd drawn. The wall I'd put up to protect myself and the strength it had taken to get this far. However, I caved, and up to this point, I'd spent the better part of 30 years trying to convince this man, my own flesh and blood, that I was good enough to be loved and to be his kid. Yet, somehow, I was still questioning my worth and value, begging for my biological father to choose me. Going from "I don't need him" to crying at night wondering, "Why didn't he need me?"

In the months following my grandfather's passing, I sought a lot of therapy and leaned into a lot of prayer. At some point, I finally drew the line in the sand and permitted myself to set a protective boundary that was necessary and not negotiable. I made it clear to my father that I had to prioritize myself because he never would. I told him I loved him, and for almost 30 years, I'd hoped he'd choose me. Not to leave his family and come get me, but to simply choose to know me, to know my kids, and be more involved in my life than just a few texts a year or when something bad happens.

That boundary was one of the toughest things I've ever done, and it was the first one I'd ever put in place and told him about. This one was different. It was a boundary I was putting into place to protect myself. It was painful, and I cried for months off and on. I was better than this. I deserved better than this.

It's been four years since I reached out and asked my father not to contact me anymore. I committed long ago to break the generational cycles and give my kids a life I never had, but now I had to put my money where my mouth was.

The buck stops here. The cycles stop with me.

Letting him back in when it suited him wasn't cutting it, and it exposed my kids to a lifestyle I didn't want for them. They saw my tears, saw me in pain, and saw the conflict it was creating inside—exactly what I said I'd never allow. I was done.

During a therapy session about a year later, after I had last reached out to my father to stop contact, I had a profound sense of realization as I was sharing my process of putting this boundary in place.

You should never have to beg for a parent's love.

So I chose me. And I've yet to look back.

Chapter 16

Unsettling Waves

After closing that chapter and intentionally reinforcing the boundary I had established for self-preservation, I recognized the importance of committing to prayer and continuing therapy. I was acutely aware that the choice I had made might lead to feelings of regret or pain that could push me into isolation, so I proactively took steps to address it. I dedicated myself to revitalizing my business and restructuring my organization. I discovered a sense of peace through worship music, reading, regular therapy sessions, and the support of close friends. My husband, a pillar of strength, provided unwavering support. At the same time, I daily acknowledged the invaluable backing of my family and a few friends, who aided in healing the wounds and pain of the past year.

Life took a sharp turn when the global pandemic hit. Changes upon changes followed. What began as a short school break became a whole year of homeschooling and juggling business challenges. Despite it all, my drive for innovation persisted. I experimented with new business approaches while finding solace in spending more time with my family on our farm. With the hustle and bustle of daily life coming to a halt, I found a rhythm in working purposefully, treasuring our sanctuary on the hill. Isolated from the world, surrounded by the mountains and close family. Boredom took over, and we added chickens, turkeys, rabbits, and goats to the farm. All of these were compulsive decisions that I regretted at some point or another. Don't tell my husband that.

With the surge in online shopping, my business took an unexpected turn, gaining momentum as I connected with more people virtually. Exploring networking groups, advertising, and social media brought new opportunities. Amid fears and losses due to the pandemic, it was a period of introspection and growth. I focused on my goals, reflecting on my purpose and deepening my spiritual practices through prayer and Bible studies.

As the world slowly reopened, I found myself grateful for the lessons learned and growth gained during this challenging time. It has taught me to adapt to change, find inner strength, and prioritize what truly matters. I've also learned the importance of self-care and taking breaks for mental health. Having worked from home for 13 years before the onset of COVID, one might assume I was well-equipped for the pandemic. Yet, the reality is that remote work demands a certain resilience. It can be isolating, especially when the freedom to attend social gatherings and events that were anticipated all year is no longer an option. The sense of isolation became more pronounced following personal upheavals and losses, threatening to engulf me. To evade this pitfall, I consciously made an effort each day to stay connected and became present in each moment, enjoying my time with my family.

Uncertain if it was the pandemic, the season of setting crucial boundaries, or a combination, there came a point in my life when I purposely started praying more specifically for God's purpose for me, looking toward my future. For over 13 years, I felt assured that I was aligned with my calling, but with deep contemplation and prayer, a stronger urge towards a grander path emerged. This new direction unsettled me, and I hesitated to pursue it because change felt daunting. Yet, an inner tug, a gut feeling, hinted at an impending season of transformation leading to a breakthrough. Although unsure of what lay ahead, I continued leading a remarkable group of women, promoting beloved products, and standing by a company, mission, and industry that resonated with my core beliefs.

Our first incentive trip post-pandemic was highly anticipated. These yearly excursions were paused during the pandemic, and a few were canceled due to hurricanes, so it had been a while since we last traveled for one. After almost 15 years in the business, I had finally achieved the top level of the trip. I was thrilled to embark on this journey, show appreciation to my team, and enjoy some well-deserved time with my husband.

Our company had faced numerous changes in the years leading up to this, including shifts in leadership. This trip was crucial in bringing us back together. We had navigated turbulent times, those gnarly white waters, leadership changes, and the challenges of the pandemic—and I longed for a sense of normalcy or at least some consistency. Plus, I missed all of my people.

What I hadn't realized was that this particular trip would signify a notable milestone in my life. While the trip was enjoyable and brimming with memories, an internal conflict weighed on me, causing unease throughout the entire week. Initially unable to pinpoint the source, upon returning to our hotel room each night, I confided in my husband, expressing, "Something feels off. I can't quite place it, but things don't seem right." Observing the interactions of both seasoned and new consultants by the pool, sharing ideas, laughter, and camaraderie, I felt like a mere spectator throughout the trip, struggling to fully engage in the moments due to the persistent disquiet within me. This particular journey felt distinct. I anticipated this trip for over a year, yet I could not discern the underlying reasons for my emotions during the experience. It felt as if I stood at the edge of a cliff, hesitating to leap into unknown waters, constantly looking back in indecision. The sensation of impending change left me apprehensive, unsure of its implications. Following turbulent developments, leadership transitions, personnel departures, and the onset of the pandemic, it became evident that the dynamics within our company had shifted, a realization that weighed heavily on me. My husband astutely noted one evening as we prepared for bed in our hotel room: "Change may not feel great, but it isn't necessarily negative. As long as the mission and core values remain unchanged, isn't that what truly matters?"

I stood there. In this vast bathroom full of marble and bright lights, I finished washing my face and just stared in the mirror. I knew this was more than just a company and great products. It was a mission. It's why I was here, why I had stayed. Why I had chosen to rebuild. For the nearly 15 years I'd been here, this was a mission field of opportunity, growth, transformation, healing, restoration, and life-changing moments. We were different, and I believed that our mission and core values were what did that. When he said this statement to me, I said out loud as I stared at myself in the mirror, "So how, as a field of leaders, do we protect the mission and core values no matter who's in the leadership roles and no matter what comes at us?"

I was uncertain of the answer, but the mere contemplation felt like a question I needed to unravel. Though I doubted my ability to resolve it or possess any unique qualities that could lead to a different outcome, I sensed the power of one individual to spark change. A single person voicing their aspirations and purpose can inspire others to follow. Unclear about the path ahead, that night I prayed, "If there's a leap I must take over a cliff I'm unsure of, I believe it involves this. I sometimes lack clarity, so please illuminate the way with a clear sign. God, I need a billboard."

We headed to the beach to lounge on a Bali bed with friends the following day. While strolling along the beach, capturing moments in pictures and soaking up the sun, a fellow leader and friend approached our spot. What began as a casual conversation transformed into a profound hour-long dialogue about her challenges in business and the uncertainty she felt about her future. She confided, "I'm praying for guidance, but I sense my time here might be ending." Moved by her pain and vulnerability, I transitioned from friend to coach. After listening intently for nearly half an hour, I felt compelled to ask probing questions and assist her in navigating her emotions and doubts. She bravely responded with tears in her eyes, and we leaned in together, offering comfort and sharing our vulnerabilities. I opened up about my own business struggles and the resilience required for my personal reset. How the challenges seemed insurmountable, leading me to question if this marked the end — if it was time for a new chapter in my life.

As we continued our conversation, I was in awe of the power of connection and vulnerability in the moment. I realized that simply being present and listening can not only offer comfort but also provide guidance and clarity. At that moment, I realized this was the leap I had prayed for the night before.

We often underestimate the impact we can have on others by sharing our own struggles and experiences. Storytelling is powerful. Vulnerability can be seen as a weakness, but it takes great strength to open up and be vulnerable to others. It allows for deeper connections, growth, and learning from one another.

In my coaching work, I have found that vulnerability is critical to breaking through barriers and achieving personal growth. It allows individuals to become more self-aware, acknowledge their emotions, and healthily work through them. It also fosters trust and understanding within relationships.

So, instead of seeing the end as a negative event, we can choose to see it as an opportunity for new beginnings—a chance to shed old ways of thinking and embrace vulnerability, paving the way for growth and transformation. As my friend discovered during our conversation, sometimes all it takes is opening up and being vulnerable to find the clarity and strength needed to take that leap of faith.

We delved into our shared passion and memories surrounding our company and its mission. Reflecting on the past, we pondered how to shape our future amidst the numerous changes we've faced. The question I posed to her mirrored my own contemplation from the previous night: "How can we, as a group of leaders who have contributed to building this business, unite to preserve our identity and uphold a legacy that fills us with pride? Our environment is unique, and countless women (and some men) are eagerly awaiting an opportunity like the one we offer. So, how can we redefine who we are and extend our reach more than ever?"

We didn't immediately find a solution, but as she got ready to leave and hugged me, her genuine sincerity deeply moved me. She said in a hushed and emotional tone, "Thank you for opening up and sharing your journey and listening to me babble about mine. You made me pause and truly reflect, not just think and react. I'm committed to making a change, one way or the other." I smiled, and as she turned away, she looked back at me and said, "But there are many others who feel like this, Hope. I wish they could all hear this message and be reminded of the belief that still thrives within you, within this mission, in our story - I hope you'll find a way to share that with others."

I returned to the bed and locked eyes with my bestie, Leslie. Her eyes welled up with tears like mine, but we simply shared a smile and blinked them away. The moment was heavy, but we didn't sit in it. We each knew how the other felt, and we were aligned on our hope for the future and our company's legacy. We also loved that fellow leader and knew that conversation was monumental, and it was one that many of our leaders probably needed to have. It felt like a shift was coming, something about to happen. As chatter continued around me, I rose to walk towards the water alone. I gazed at the ocean, took a deep breath, and just like that, that impending pull I'd felt for quite some time, explicitly leading into this trip, made itself known.

Like the ebb and flow of capricious waves, it left me feeling unsettled.

Chapter 17

Clarity Emerges

During the plane journey home, I confronted the internal shift within me. On my way back, I acknowledged the deep-seated uncertainty and restlessness I had been feeling. Having dedicated nearly 15 years to building a thriving million-dollar empire from the ground up, climbing to the pinnacle of the corporate ladder, and navigating through successes and setbacks, I found myself at a pivotal juncture I wasn't prepared for. I had a lot to be proud of: advocating for our industry at the Capitol, advancing our business's mission, becoming a certified coach to nurture my team's growth, and shaping a legacy I was proud of. Yet, amidst my accomplishments, I realized that my tenure as a national sales leader was drawing to a close, a realization that caught me off guard. While relishing the flexibility and autonomy of entrepreneurship in our industry, the notion of leaving it all behind seemed unfathomable. Nevertheless, a robust inner calling compelled me to consider a transition from my current role, carrying forth my skills, knowledge, expertise, and enthusiasm to the corporate realm of our business.

The dilemma lay in the rarity of businesses promoting top-level leaders from the field to corporate roles. Such transitions were uncommon, with most leaders opting to switch companies to pursue a corporate career or climb the ladder elsewhere. This reality instilled fear in me, as my entire career had been within a single company since my early twenties. Despite grappling with this inner conflict, the persistent calling grew louder and more precise, overwhelming me to the point of sickness and many restless nights.

The thought of leaving behind a team I had spent 15 years nurturing, along with the relationships I cherished – my very legacy – weighed heavily on me. I took pride in the organization I had crafted, the leaders I had mentored, and the collective mission we embodied. Could I genuinely walk away from everything I had built to embrace a corporate role, a realm of employment I had previously shunned? It was a wild consideration.

All of it felt overwhelming - the mere idea, the initial steps, and the thought of confiding in anyone about it. The weight of needing to make a decision was suffocating. Doubts plagued my mind - questioning my intelligence, competence, and qualifications for such a role. I grappled with the uncertainty of whether any company, let alone mine, would consider me worthy of such a position. I accepted the challenge, understanding the importance of answering this calling, even though my time as a leader was drawing to a close.

The future may have been uncertain, but I embraced each step and decision with trust in a God I knew had instilled a dream inside me. I prayed for an opportunity to discuss this with the right individuals, wondering if it was a viable option. I even explored opportunities in other companies, seeking feedback on how my active leadership would be perceived. Before deciding, I sought to understand how industry leaders viewed the prospect of someone with my experience and skills. What I found was both encouraging and disheartening.

As I delved into the corporate world of my beloved industry, it became clear that there was a lack of representation from those with hands-on experience. The absence of individuals who had effectively led organizations and participated in sales, networking, and recruitment activities was striking. While many business owners and high-level executives possessed such experience, I noticed a gap in the area I am most passionate about: training & coaching. While some had industry expertise to share, there was a distinction between knowing what to do and actively engaging in the do process. I've had the privilege of working with remarkable development coaches and trainers with extensive knowledge and a genuine desire to support others in their growth within this industry. Yet, I've recognized the importance of having a perspective within the company from an individual actively involved in its development. This presence can significantly enhance training, programs, communications, and the decision-making processes.

During discussions with other companies and industry coaches I'd contacted in confidence, it became clear that my aspiration to transition from my current role and bring my passion and skills to the corporate world was not a common choice. I was even told that mine was unique because of my distinct passion for the company I'd grown up with, which is unheard of these days. This was more than just a job to me. It was a calling.

Despite my fear of rejection and the lessons learned in just a few weeks, as I questioned the validity of my situation, I rose with conviction that this opportunity was unique to my current company, with faith that God had already laid out the path. Why not have trust in it? My objective was crystal clear: I sensed a calling to depart from my current field, step away from my current organization, and venture into the corporate realm. My mission was to propel our purpose, to bring about a substantial influence by building a connection between the corporate sphere and the field, fostering a collaborative partnership, and spearheading the envisioned transformation we discussed on that day by the beach. Not because I believed I possessed unmatched qualities but because I believed my perspective, experience, and fervor were indispensable. By facing my fear of rejection, I believed that if a higher purpose guided this journey, the path ahead would reveal itself.

With nervousness running through my veins, I finally took the conversation to my current sales officer and shared my heart and this newfound calling on my life. God must have been paving a path elsewhere, if not with my current company, and I had to take a step to figure it out. She shared with me that a position was coming up on the team, and she felt this conversation should continue with our CEO.

That was in May of 2022, just a little over a month since our incentive trip.

Unbeknownst to me, I received an overwhelming amount of support, love, and validation. My purpose became clear like the sun breaking through the clouds after a fierce storm. In June 2022, I accepted a role on the corporate sales team at my current company, guiding the field through training, coaching, and program development.

Like a nurturing mother bird coaxing her babies to take flight, I bid a fond farewell to my team as their resolute leader. I challenged them to carry forth my legacy by embodying all I had imparted to them, knowing that this decision was more about their growth and future at this company than mine. In a season dedicated to service, despite the daunting prospect of departure and what that meant for me, I was unwaveringly confident that it was precisely the path I was destined to tread.

Most of my leader peers welcomed me and embraced the changes this would bring to the business. While some may have hesitated about the decision initially, the overwhelming support and affection I received from my cherished field confirmed that this path was right for me. Joining the corporate team led me to forge deep friendships, find my biggest supporters, and be pushed to improve daily. My colleagues embraced me and challenged me in so many ways. As I now get closer to my second anniversary on the corporate team, I've grown by leaps and bounds, even tapping into new passions and talents I was unaware of.

As we progress, I reflect on my 15-year journey with gratitude and purpose. This intentional path has brought healing, restoration, and a sense of identity and direction into my life. This journey has been instrumental in shaping me into the compassionate leader, educator, and coach I am today. It entered my life when my daughter fell ill, made possible by another woman who took a bold step, clearing a path for me.

Purchasing that vibrant $99 enrollment kit unlocked a transformative path that has been nothing short of remarkable. It has not only defined my career but has also enriched my personal life, influencing my role as a wife, mother, and Christian. This business has been my foundation, shaping me into the individual I am proud to be today. I am privileged to wake up each morning with the opportunity to contribute to its growth and impact and give back to it daily.

This journey has not only enriched my life but also ignited a passion within me to carry forward this industry's legacy. I am dedicated to encouraging individuals from all walks of life to experience this transformative path, one that has been pivotal in my growth and development.

I embrace my passions and expertise through crafting training programs, coaching workshops, and championing our industry from enrollment to leadership development. Collaborating with an exceptional team, guided by a visionary CEO who transformed my life, I am privileged to work alongside her, sharing dreams and aspirations.

As I continue to navigate this journey, I am reminded of the power of mentorship and community. Through my personal experiences, I have learned the importance of having a strong support system and role models who inspire and guide you each step of the way. This is why I prioritize paying it forward and providing mentorship and guidance to individuals, even letting some borrow my belief in them until they discover it themselves.

So what happens from here?

The narrative unfolds and progresses, an ongoing tale with chapters yet to be penned. My ambition drives me to ascend the corporate ranks in this industry, appreciating every step, decision, and moment that brought me to this point. I'm eternally grateful for the journey and excited about the future.

Chapter 18

Beauty From Ashes

Looking back on my life's journey, it's evident that each challenge and triumph has molded me into a resilient individual. From a childhood marked by pain and neglect, to my teenage years seeking unconditional love, and transitioning into motherhood and marriage while evading a haunting past - and finally emerging as a businesswoman compelled to chase a bright future, I've had to learn how to keep going. I've unearthed my purpose and the fighter within me by rebuilding my business, navigating family dynamics, salvaging my marriage, and rediscovering strength through faith. These experiences have imparted invaluable lessons that I carry daily, empowering me to surmount any obstacle and emerge even stronger than before.

In the quiet moments of reflection, I've come to recognize the profound metamorphosis that's taken place within me — a transformation only possible by allowing divine intervention to take root in the deepest recesses of my soul. It's a transformation akin to the Biblical promise of God granting "beauty from ashes," a metaphor resonating deeply with my own experiences. This process wasn't instantaneous, nor was it without its trials. Yet, through these very struggles, I found my purpose and established my worth, and the path to true healing began to unveil itself, illuminated by faith.

There was a time when the metaphorical ashes of my past seemed too dense to sift through – the remnants of loss, pain, and despair seemingly insurmountable. However, in my darkest moments, when hope flickered faintly like the last ember in a dying fire, I found solace in the possibility of redemption and the strength to surrender to a power greater than my own. This surrender was not a sign of weakness but rather the first step in acknowledging that within the divine plan, there is a purpose for every tear shed, every moment of suffering, and every obstacle encountered.

Through God's grace, it became evident that my ashes were not the sign of the end but the beginning. The scars that I bore, both physical and emotional, started to symbolize not just my survival but my ability to thrive despite adversity. They were reminders of resilience; in them, I found the most unexpected opportunities for growth and transformation. Like the woman at the well, my deepest wounds were being healed, and beauty was being cultivated in their place.

God's work within us often mirrors the processes we see in nature – silent yet profound, gradual yet persistent. Just as the most rugged landscapes can give birth to the most breathtaking vistas, our most difficult experiences can also yield extraordinary outcomes when we allow God to work through our lives. In surrendering to Him, I eventually found freedom; in my weakness, I discovered His strength; and in my brokenness, I was made whole. This was the beauty from ashes, a testament to the unfathomable depths of divine love and the miraculous ways in which it can transform our lives.

Through this ongoing spiritual journey, I've unearthed a sense of purpose that transcends the accumulation of personal achievements or material success. It's a purpose rooted in compassion, resilience, and the unwavering belief in the possibility of redemption. Each day presents a new opportunity to be a beacon of hope for others, to share the lessons learned from my trials, and to demonstrate that with faith, no circumstance is too dire, no pain too deep, and no mistake too great to be transformed into something truly beautiful.

This next chapter of my life, filled with newfound purpose and opportunities, still stands as a beacon not just for me but for anyone who feels weighed down by their past. It's a testament to the power of faith to heal, transform, and reveal the hidden treasures within us all, waiting to be discovered when we open our hearts to God's calling on our lives.

In this process of transformation, it's important to acknowledge the one barrier I struggled to get through more than others. Finding the strength to forgive. Forgiving others was a mountain to climb, but forgiving myself felt like scaling an insurmountable peak. Yet, once I embraced the full extent of God's grace, I understood that forgiveness wasn't about erasing the past but about permitting myself to heal and move forward. It became clear that to love who I am genuinely, scars included, required an act of unexplainable strength that could only come from letting God work within my heart.

This intentional path of forgiveness has been pivotal in rebuilding my faith and my heart, body, mind, and soul. It's as though each act of forgiveness is a brick laid on the foundation of a renewed spirit. With every step taken in faith, I can feel my soul being stitched back together, stronger and more resilient than before. This isn't a mere return to who I was before the ashes; it's an evolution into who I'm meant to be — sculpted by grace, perseverance, and an unwavering belief in the power of redemption. It was the freedom that no person in my past or future could have control of my story anymore and that my voice was mine to own. My story was mine to tell. It was a story of God's overwhelming, never-ending, reckless love of God.

As I continue to walk this path, I am reminded that beauty from ashes isn't just a one-time event with a beautiful ending but an ongoing process. It's a journey of self-discovery, growth, and transformation that never truly ends. Each day brings new challenges and opportunities for healing and forgiveness; the more I embrace them, the more beautiful my life becomes.

So, if you find yourself amid ashes, know this is not the end. It's only the beginning of a beautiful new chapter waiting to be written. Embrace the weakness of being so broken that all you have left is Him. He stood in my pit of rock bottom, in my dark cave of escape. Leaving the 99 and coming back for me. That is the God I serve, and it's God I handed my broken heart, my feeble body, and my battered mind to and let all my guards down, knowing there was nothing left to lose. That same God will come for you. That same God will fight for you.

Looking back over my life, one of my greatest realizations was the understanding that my transformation was not solely for my own healing; it became clear that it was crucial for breaking the generational curses that had ensnared my family lineage. From the outset, I recognized that, without intervention, these cycles of pain and suffering would perpetuate and inevitably taint the futures of my children. As I matured, I started comprehending the profound secrets hidden within my own family, and the realization that I was the victim of unbroken cycles from generations past weighed on my heart. Within this realization, there was no room for blame or resentment, only a profound sense of responsibility and even sadness for the others before me who had yet to encounter this or encountered it late in life. From the start, I was determined to shield my children from the hardships I endured. It wasn't just about providing a stable home; as a mother, it meant confronting hidden trauma rather than burying it, allowing myself the chance to heal. Ignoring it only sets the stage for it to resurface, potentially tearing families apart. Whenever I felt like giving up, or the therapy was too hard, the tears were too much, or the pain was too fresh, thoughts of my kids' faces reminded me that I had to face this head-on for their sake. The buck stops here.

Though imperfectly undertaken, the act of breaking these curses was imbued with the intention to mend what was broken and to forge a new legacy defined by freedom, health, and spiritual wholeness. This endeavor was not about rewriting the past; instead, it was about reshaping the future. By confronting and overcoming these inherited burdens, I was not only liberating myself but also ensuring that my children, and their children after them, would be free to live lives unencumbered by the shadows of ancestral woes.

The deep, inner work of mending my own wounds allowed me to step back into motherhood with a level of consciousness and presence I might not have otherwise achieved as my kids were getting older. While I wish I'd done all this work before becoming a mother, I now see it happened just in time, in God's time. This personal evolution was about healing myself and how I showed up every day for my children. I was determined to parent from a place of healed scars rather than open wounds, to offer them the stability and emotional safety I had to fight so hard to give myself.

My healing became the lens through which I viewed each parenting decision, big or small. It was personal in every shared bedtime story, conflict resolved, and moment of joy celebrated. I was more patient and willing to listen and engage deeply with their thoughts and feelings. My experiences taught me the value of true empathy and understanding, which I aim to embody daily. In doing so, I hoped to nurture their minds, bodies, and spirits. I spent most of my life looking for a safe place and was looking for it in all the wrong places, so when it came to my kids...I wanted to be theirs.

This new approach to parenting has inspired me to cultivate an environment where open communication thrives and seeking help, whether emotional or otherwise, is viewed as a strength rather than a weakness. My goal has been to nurture my children with the emotional intelligence and resilience needed to confront their own challenges. While I offer guidance and support, I understand that their journeys are uniquely their own. As my kids transition into their teenage years, I am immensely thankful that my efforts have allowed me to authentically connect with them, fostering genuine friendships and providing a secure haven for them to rely on.

By breaking the chains of past traumas and modeling a continuous growth and healing life, I aspired to give them the freedom to carve out lives rich with purpose, joy, and love, unburdened by the shadows of generational pain. It was the most personal and profound way I could show up for them, shaping how I nurtured, guided, and loved them through each phase of their lives.

I often gaze at them and ponder how proud I am of the outstanding individuals they've become. My daughter, my firstborn, mirrors me but in a more remarkable way. She has become my very best friend, and I refuse to believe she'll ever leave me. She embodies determination, independence, beauty, a vibrant passion for life, an attitude, and a strong stance on what she believes. As for my son, he will forever be my little one, a constant source of kindness and compassion, serving as a reminder of the depth of God's boundless love. That child possesses a heart as vast as Texas, brimming with empathy. Regardless of the day's challenges, he faithfully immerses himself in the Bible each night and never fails to hug and kiss me before bed. He better hope he doesn't grow out of that all the way. I could fill pages for days about what these two have given me and how they helped heal me. As children, I'm sure they often believe they need me more than I need them, but they are the reason I get up each day and the reason I keep pressing on when I don't feel like it. I feel honored and overwhelmingly grateful to be their mom and watch their lives unfold.

I never imagined I could create a life like this. It's far from perfect, with daily challenges, but at its core are two young lovers who married quickly and journeyed through life together. One stumbled often, while the other offered support, both emerging stronger, wiser, and thankful on the other side. As a result, there are now two more exceptional individuals to make the world better.

Beauty from ashes.

Chapter 19

Circle of Trust

Throughout my life, the concept of friendship had often felt like an enigma, wrapped in layers of mistrust and past hurts. My history with friendships was marked by caution, a self-imposed isolation that kept me at arm's length from potential heartaches. The scars of being betrayed more times than I could recall conditioned me to guard my heart fiercely, allowing very few to breach the walls I had meticulously built. This protective barrier extended beyond personal life into the professional realm, where my inner circle remained tightly sealed despite my role connecting me with thousands of women consistently.

However, the universe had a plan unbeknownst to me that would challenge my preconceived notions about friendships and bless me with a treasure I had longed for all my life. It was back in 2012, amid my professional endeavors, that our paths crossed. She was someone I was meant to mentor, a bright and eager young woman who joined my team, her career just starting. She was a teacher looking to grow her income, and her bubbly personality revealed a thriving customer base. What began as a mentor-mentee relationship, based on professional growth and achievement, gradually and almost imperceptibly evolved into something profoundly deeper.

Our connection transcended the typical boundaries of work. It was as if the universe conspired to answer my silent prayers for a genuine friend—a soul sister with whom silence spoke volumes, and laughter was abundant. Our friendship wasn't instantaneous; it was a gradual unveiling, a delicate dance of trust-building and shared experiences. With her, I rediscovered the joys of uninhibited laughter, the comfort of shared silences, and the strength of vulnerability. She became the mirror reflecting the parts of me I had forgotten, reminding me that trust, once shattered, could be rebuilt.

This friendship transformed me, softening the edges of my skepticism and illuminating the landscape of my life with the warmth of genuine connection. She was the unexpected gift, the soul sister I had yearned for, proving that even the most guarded hearts could find a haven in the genuine bond of friendship. Through her, I learned that while past wounds might shape us, they don't have to define our capacity for connection and love. Our friendship, born out of professional ties, bloomed into a life-changing force, teaching me the invaluable lesson that sometimes, the most impactful relationships are the ones we least expect.

Leslie radiates a vibrant zest for life that enveloped me. Her passion for travel, positive attitude, and genuine love for others unveiled a whole new world when I embraced life through her eyes. With a lighthearted perspective, she injected joy into my struggling career during those challenging years. Although I have only briefly mentioned her in my journey, her presence in my life was pivotal and helped shape me into who I am today. Although absent during darker times, she arrived at the perfect moment to uplift me and has remained a steadfast companion ever since. She is privy to every facet of my life, a confidante I trust implicitly with everything. Hence, it feels only appropriate to dedicate this space to her, an entire chapter as a tribute to her profound impact on my life.

We often hear about how important it is to surround ourselves with positive and supportive people. However, Leslie showed me that it's not just about having people who support us but also those who challenge us and push us outside our comfort zones. She encouraged me to take risks and pursue my passions, even when I doubted myself. She believed in me when I didn't believe in myself and pushed me to be the best version of myself.

Leslie also taught me the beauty of vulnerability and authenticity in relationships. Her openness and willingness to share her struggles and successes showed me that true connection can only be formed through honesty and genuine communication. Our friendship is where you can drop by unannounced, lend a hand tidying up the house, or snuggle up in bed all day watching crime movies. My dearest adventures, memories, and important moments are intertwined with her, and I'm grateful for that.

I've been privileged to witness her transformation into a wife, a mother, a business owner, and a leader. The pride I feel for her is indescribable. Our families have intertwined at the core, and I see them as nothing less than my own. Despite the distance in our zip codes, our friendship thrives, a daily reminder of our precious bond and our profound influence in each other's lives.

During one of my darkest days, following the loss of my grandfather and while navigating the challenges in my relationship with my father, I reached out to her in tears, seeking to maintain a healthy state of mind. Needing some friend therapy, the kind where someone just listens. The following day, I was surprised to find her holding her son in her arms at my doorstep. She'd made the two-hour drive to wrap her arms around me and when her son ran to embrace me, broken parts of me were already mending. We spent the entire day together without specific plans, just being in each other's company. Moments like these reminded me of the true essence of a soul sister - someone who willingly chooses to stand by your side through the tough times. Yet, also force you to put one foot in front of the other when you don't feel capable. A friendship where you don't question how they feel, or if they talk behind your back, or wonder if they'll show up for you. This is the friendship I needed but didn't know existed.

Through our friendship, I've learned the importance of having someone who can both comfort and challenge you—someone who can be your confidant and your cheerleader all at once. It's a rare gift to find in a friend, and I'm grateful daily for her presence in my life.

She may not realize the profound impact she has had on me. She serves as a constant reminder that I am worthy in all aspects of my life and deserve nothing but the best. When I confided in her about my career choice, she was among the first to know before anyone else on my team. Her pride in me and her genuine concern for my well-being were her only priorities. Everyone needs a friend like her, someone who stands by you, protects you, and always has your back. Despite distance or time apart, she remains steadfast in her support and willingness to be there for me.

In a world constantly bombarded with messages about self-care and self-love, it's easy to forget the importance of having a strong support system. Having a true, genuine friend, someone who truly understands and accepts you for who you are, can make all the difference in navigating life's challenges. They provide a sense of comfort and security that allows us to be our most authentic selves.

All of my life, I thought the more friends, the better. The larger the circle, the better. Then, as my daughter navigates that journey herself, I'm reminded that that isn't always the case. One true friend is better than five that you hope are your friends. Throughout my healing journey, I had to end relationships I thought were precious and pure because I later realized they weren't healthy for me, and I didn't like who I was when I was with them.

My close circle may seem small to some, but it's a safe haven to me. It's not just about having supportive people around you; it's about having those who lift you when you stumble. I've found that kind of support in my husband, parents, sister, Leslie, my in-laws, and a few others. It's crucial to be vulnerable enough for others to truly see and understand you so they can offer genuine help. Sometimes, I felt utterly alone and isolated, mostly because I had shut people out. I acknowledge that only some have a strong support system, and I empathize with that. It's challenging to navigate difficulties alone. So, if you find yourself in that place of loneliness and isolation, I want to empower you to borrow some of my belief in you - that you are worthy and capable of healing. I hope this book will foster a community of women who uplift each other and show up as their authentic selves. From all walks of life across the globe, women share a unique connection that we all need from time to time. This friendship played a significant role in my healing journey. Had I not been vulnerable and open enough to experience and let someone from the outside in, I worry about the progress I would have made or who I may have turned out to be.

True friendship is a universal language that knows no boundaries. It's not limited by race, ethnicity, culture, or even distance. In today's digital age, we have the opportunity to connect with individuals from all over the world and create meaningful friendships that transcend physical barriers. Social media platforms like Instagram and Facebook allow us to stay in touch with old friends and make new ones, expanding our support system and providing us with a sense of belonging.

Social media can be used for good at times. When people step out to share stories, specifically women, there is a miraculous movement that takes place, and I want to use this part of my story to inspire you to step out and look for it. Or if you have it, do not take advantage of it and protect it.

Authentic friendships involve open and honest communication, empathy, trust, and support. It's about being there for each other during the good and bad, celebrating each other's successes, lifting each other during challenging moments, and wanting the other to win, even if it means beating you. It requires you to show up without any masks or pretenses. In a world that often pressures us to conform and fit in, true friendships provide a safe space to be our true, unapologetic selves. It's about finding those people who appreciate and support us for who we are, flaws and all.

So, when your pals go quiet, give them a shout. When they score a win, celebrate with them. When they crave space, just be there quietly. And when you feel like a night out, stop talking about it—make plans for it instead. If you see another female out and love her makeup, tell her. If her smile brings you joy, affirm her by sharing that she lights up a room.

There is power in solidarity and support, especially for those who have faced trauma or adversity. By lifting each other and standing together, we can create an unbreakable community of resilience and empowerment.

I encourage you to cultivate a circle of trust or safeguard the one you've established without measuring it against others. My personal journey is just one tale among many that can ignite healing, foster connections, and promote authentic acceptance in a world that can sometimes make us feel isolated by convincing us we are alone. Share your stories, embrace your truth, lend an ear to others, and allow yourself to discover a supportive community that can surround you in each step of your journey.

Dear Leslie,

Reflecting on our friendship, my heart is brimming with gratitude and memories that dance vividly in my mind, painting a picture of countless shared moments that have shaped the fabric of our friendship. It's these moments, both big and small, that have compelled me to put pen to paper and attempt to capture the essence of what you mean to me.
I often find myself thinking back to the day you surprised me with a visit to the Warner Bros Studios to explore the set of Friends. Despite having experienced it yourself, the sheer joy and excitement you exhibited for me was a testament to your selflessness and your unparalleled capacity to find happiness in my happiness. It was a day that spoke volumes, not just about our shared love for coffee and laughter, but about the depth of your friendship and love for me.
Then there was the time I held your newborn, a tiny bundle of joy, sleeping peacefully on the couch while you moved around, attending to the endless list of chores. In that moment, as I watched you, a vision of strength and grace, I couldn't help but feel overwhelmed by the trust and bond between us. Through all the laughter, the late-night walks through the bustling streets of NYC, our crime movie marathons, or those nights of wine and dancing in your kitchen or lounging in bed ordering room service - you've been my rock, my soul sister, and my beacon of hope.
Leslie, your zest for life is infectious; your passion for others, boundless. You possess a heart of gold, always putting others before yourself, always ready to lend an ear or a shoulder to lean on. In you, I have found more than a friend - I've found a sister, a guardian, and a soul so incredibly beautiful, words fall short of capturing your essence.

Thank you. Thank you for showing me the true meaning of friendship and connection. Thank you for the grace, understanding, and unwavering support you've showered upon me throughout our journey. Your mere presence in my life has been a source of constant comfort and joy. You've celebrated my victories as if they were your own, provided solace during my defeats, and have loved me and my family unconditionally. Leslie, you are my circle of trust, my cheerleader, and, most importantly, my person.

As we continue to weave new memories and share more of life's journeys, know that your friendship is a treasure I hold dear, a gift I cherish deeply. Here's to more laughter, more adventures, and countless moments that leave us breathless with joy.

I seriously love the fire out of you.
- Hopey

Hope & Leslie
April 2023

Chapter 20

You Are Enough

In 2016, I received a book from our company's CEO - "The Traveler's Gift" by Andy Andrews. It's been my go-to guide in navigating my personal and professional journey ever since. Reading it twice yearly grounds me and helps me stay focused; it helps me stay on my path of healing and reminds me that perspective is everything. The story follows a man who time-travels, learning essential life lessons from historical figures and ultimately altering his future by challenging him to change his perspective on life. Each chapter walks you through 7 decisions this man made to shift his mindset and outlook on situations he didn't have control over. It's not about what happens to you but how you react to what happens to you.

This book has profoundly influenced me, shaping my approach to each season of life and engraining those seven decisions in my head. I often reflect on specific chapters and imagine the scene, reminding myself that no matter how complex the challenge, pain, or situation, I must step back and respond versus react. I always tell my kids, "Reaction typically occurs out of emotion. Response occurs from reflection and pause. Be smart in how you reply to things people say to you, how they treat you, and the things that life will throw your way."

So why am I sharing this book with you? If you know me personally, I mention it in many conversations. Whether it's in a coaching conversation, building training content, helping a friend through a challenging season, or just reflecting on a great book- it's one that I've tucked deep into my soul. It resonated so deeply with me that I brought the "seven decisions" list to my first therapy session years ago and used them to share my story over nearly a year of sessions. While I haven't time traveled, each scene from the book, each chapter, each lesson, and each decision reminded me of my own life. It challenged me to reflect on my journey and make a decision along my healing journey as to how I would choose to respond to each chapter of my own.

Throughout my life, I've encountered various forms of destruction—some physical, some emotional, and some that have shattered my perception of who I am. My story, like many others, is punctuated by chapters of trauma, rejection, fear & an unstable foundation. It's a narrative of childhood upheaval, a tale woven with threads of pain, hurt, and regret. Yet, it is also a story of healing, restoration, and, ultimately, renewal.

Finding life after trauma is akin to sifting through ruins after a calamity. Everything seems irreparable, devastatingly altered. However, within this desolation, we discover our most profound truth: our unyielding spirit and an innate desire to rise above our circumstances. To see what there is to learn amidst the rubble and choose how we want to rise from it.

After reading the book on repeat for the last seven years and having the incredible opportunity to learn from the Author himself, I will say that I believe he's presented these decisions for readers to interpret: no matter what life throws at us, we have a decision to make. Will it define us, or could it potentially deliver us?

This book prompts me to contemplate the advice I would offer my 10-year-old self today or what wisdom I might impart to the 20-year-old who ventured into a sales business armed only with hope and not experience. The book's core message is the power of our decisions. We cannot control what life throws at us, and while sometimes our own choices and behaviors can bring us situations that are less than ideal or maybe incredible opportunities, we are not in control. It's up to us to decide how to respond and tap into what we can learn from each season of life and what to do with the story of life, even when we don't like it.

Looking back over my journey, I can confidently say that I spent more than half of it running from my story, dismissing chapters, and burying pain in a place I hoped no one could see. Somewhere along the way, God began to use a business, people, and situations in my life to get my attention and attempt to mend my broken soul. Each time, I had a decision to make. I could ignore it, reject it, run from it, or reposition myself to say, "Maybe I really am good enough to change the course of my life and write a new future." Not feeling worthy, strong, or loved enough for so long can play with your head and heart into believing you deserve anything better than the cards you've been dealt. That you'll never heal, love, recover, sleep well again, or be able to stand in confidence. You see, long before we find our confidence, our courage, or even our voice, we face a fundamental question: Am I enough? That was the lingering question for so long. Do I deserve healing?

Let's acknowledge that each of us has faced insecurity at some point in our lives, and often, that question arises when we're faced with a difficult decision or challenge. We doubt if we have what it takes to succeed - the skills, the knowledge, the experience. But here's the thing: you are enough. You always have been. I ran across a quote once in my 20s, a sign in a bathroom at a boutique that read, "How cool is that the same

God that created the mountains, oceans, and galaxies looked at you and thought the world needed one of you too."

Growing up in church, I heard the scripture. I knew I had been fearfully and wonderfully made. However, I often wondered where the God that I was taught to love was. The one that loved me so much to send His son to die for me, yet would allow my father to shame me, a stepfather to hurt me, and years of pain inflicted on my momma, sister, and myself? That was the same God that said I was enough?

In this search for understanding, I've also discovered a space for growth and a flicker of hope — a possibility that perhaps the very questioning is part of a more extensive, more complex process of healing and finding meaning beyond the scars. God's plan for us was to live an abundant and fruitful life until man's first sin. Indeed, my pain and mistreatment weren't an act of God but rather a result of man's sin. I believe He crafted a plan that would require me to give my life entirely to Him and allow Him to heal me from the inside out. He was writing a story I wanted so desperately to know the ending of; instead, I realized all the questions I had...

"Does He love me?"
"Do I have a father?"
"Will anyone believe me?"
"Where is my God?"
"Am I forgiven?"
"Am I enough?"

The answers were intertwined in the chapters of my life. Sometimes obvious and other times hard to detect, but they were there. He was crafting a version of me that could only be restored through His love, His calling, and His purpose. I am overwhelmed when I really sit and think about it....

"You are the potter. I am the clay."
We are the work of HIS hands.

Each day, you hold the power to shape your experiences based on your outlook and choices. It doesn't mean crap won't happen, pain won't occur, or tribulation won't come. I've found great assurance in knowing that no matter how helpless I feel, I am the only one who can decide to still rise. I am the only one who can do the work to choose to step forward, and I'm the only one who can seek God's purpose in my life when it feels like there is none.

While I've clung to God's word, studied His Scripture, and lingered in worship, I know that Andy Andrews's book was a tool for me and allowed me to think about how I navigate things in my personal and professional life, my perspective. Having control of your response to things that happen to you can help elude the fear or anxiety that creeps in. For years, I've reflected on Andy's book, which served as a compass, reminding me of the significance of my choices in a world where I can't control what happens.

In "The Traveler's Gift" by Andy Andrews, The Seven Decisions That Determine Personal Success serve as a guiding framework for personal development and realization of one's potential. Each decision emphasizes a core principle aimed at empowering individuals to take deliberate steps toward crafting the life they desire. This compilation of wisdom is a call to action and a reminder of the power of choice in shaping our destiny, and we must take action. I know that in my personal and professional life, just wanting something isn't enough. WE MUST TAKE ACTION!

In my own words, I want to share what each decision has meant for me in this journey.

1. **The Buck Stops Here:** This decision underscores the importance of personal accountability. It teaches that individuals have control over their actions and responses to situations, urging them to take responsibility and action.

This decision was very personal to me. I decided that change would start here, with me.

2. **I Will Seek Wisdom:** This principle emphasizes the value of actively pursuing knowledge and insight, not just from books and sources of information but also through counsel from those who have experienced success and failure. It advocates for the cultivation of discernment and learning from the world around us. This means I must be willing to open up, share my story, and connect with others for insight, support, and guidance.
3. **I Am a Person of Action:** This decision champions the virtue of initiative and courage in moving toward one's goals. It encourages breaking procrastination's chains and taking bold steps, even in the face of fear or uncertainty, to turn dreams and ambitions into reality. This decision grounded me in always moving forward, even when I fell flat on my face. My why and my goals were non-negotiable, and I was prepared to do the work.
4. **I Have a Decided Heart:** This decision concerns the power of commitment and making definitive choices. It involves overcoming doubts and indecision, setting a clear direction for one's life, and pursuing unwavering conviction. This decision is my favorite. It represents my hope, even when I felt like giving up on my business or even my marriage. Despite facing challenges, I made a firm commitment to follow my heart. Even when nothing else seemed to work, my unwavering love and passion provided the strength needed to overcome dark and lonely days.
5. **Today, I Choose to Be Happy:** Happiness is presented as a choice, not a result of circumstances. This principle teaches that one's joy should not be contingent on external factors but rather a deliberate stance to remain positive and grateful despite challenges.

6. **I Will Forgive Myself:** It underlines the importance of self-forgiveness in personal growth and happiness. Recognizing that everyone makes mistakes, this decision helps release the burden of past errors, paving the way for reconciliation with oneself and others.
7. **I Will Persist Without Exception:** This final decision is about the essence of perseverance. It motivates individuals to continue striving toward their goals, regardless of obstacles, with steadfast determination, embodying the belief that relentless effort will ultimately culminate in achieving success.

These decisions have often anchored me throughout my journey, constantly reminding me that progress is made one step at a time. It may not always be flawless or picturesque, but I stand resilient. Reflecting on my path, I acknowledge that despite the challenges and painful moments, they have contributed to shaping the person I am today. I am confident in my worthiness of God's love and grace. I will dedicate my life to embracing the certainty that I am complete, regardless of others' opinions, affection, or perceptions of me. Their viewpoints are their concern, not mine. I will embrace my authentic self and continue to trust that God has a plan for my life. I choose to be happy, forgive myself, and persist without exception because they are the decisions that bring me inner peace and allow me to live in alignment with my values and purpose. My journey is not over, but with these choices as my foundation and God as my pilot, I am confident that I can overcome any obstacle and continue to grow, learn, and thrive in all areas of my life.

Throughout my story, we've witnessed how our daily choices shape our lives and affect us and those around us. As a parent, remember that your decisions significantly impact your children and the paths they will follow. As an individual, be mindful of how you treat others and the presence you bring, as it can influence every aspect of their lives. As a businesswoman, remember that your choices will chart your course, requiring you to make daily decisions that either steer you toward your goals or deter you. Just as a single drop of water creates ripples in a pond, our actions and choices have far-reaching consequences.

For years, I believed my story wasn't worth sharing until, one day, I realized it was mine to tell. I aspire to speak for those who struggle to voice their own experiences. Once a shattered soul in darkness, a sales opportunity unexpectedly became the key to unlocking my heart and dismantling the barriers I had meticulously built around me. God showered me with love, grace, and acceptance, empowering me to embrace a calling that validates my worth but also provides a platform to inspire countless others.

As we draw near this narrative's end, remember that your story, much like mine, is far from over. Each day presents a new page, an opportunity to write a new chapter filled with growth, courage, and resilience. The road to reclaiming your self-worth and navigating the vulnerabilities of life is not a straight path—it is fraught with setbacks and victories, each teaching us invaluable lessons about who we are, who we can become, and how we can decide to move forward.

You are enough. I am enough. Just as we are, in our imperfections, in our struggles, and in our triumphs. We possess an inner light that can guide us through the darkest times, a strength in our spirit. I encourage you not to shy away from your vulnerability; it is the crucible through which your true self is forged and revealed. Doing so unlocked a turn in my journey that charted the course to healing for me. Live purposefully, making choices that align with your deepest values and aspirations. Tell your stories, claim your voice, and embrace those around you who also need that reminder. It is in this authentic way of living that your worth is not just reclaimed but also celebrated.

My friends.
We are the work of HIS hands.

So yeah, we are enough.

Letters

My dearest Braylee and Austin,

I write this letter with a heart full of love for both of you, but the words seem too small to contain it. Yet, I hope to capture just a fraction of the immense joy and gratitude I feel being your mom. In every laughter, every challenge, and every quiet moment we share, I find countless blessings and lessons you've both unknowingly taught me.

Braylee, my beautiful firstborn, I sometimes think you bore the brunt of my learning curve - learning to balance being a mother, an adult, and a business leader all at once. Despite this, you have extended to me a grace beyond what I deserve. From the challenging toddler who knew how to test me, you've blossomed into an exceptionally compassionate, independent, and joyful young woman. You are nothing short of remarkable. Your humor, fearlessness, and unwavering kindness are my daily inspirations. The light you carry within you persuades me to push forward, to see the brighter side of life, and to dismiss the noise of others' judgments. Thank you for instilling in me a profound sense of purpose. Your early years were not just the beginning of your life but also the start of a transformative chapter in mine.

And Austin, my tender-hearted boy, you will forever hold a piece of my heart. There is something truly special about the bond of a mother and son, and I felt it the moment you were born. I will never forget those mid-day naps where you'd scoot up against me, and you would say, "Momma, we fit together like puzzle pieces." Those simple yet profound words reminded *me of the precious gift of being your mother. Your expansive heart, deep-seated wish to follow Christ, and compassion for others call on me to pause and appreciate the beauty of our lives. Your laughter, your smile, and your hugs are treasures I hold dear, reminding me of the joy and privilege it is to be your mom. Seeing your father's reflection in you makes my heart swell with gratitude.*

To both of you, as you forge ahead in your journeys, my deepest desire is for you never to question your value. You are uniquely designed for the incredible lives you lead. I pray for you to embody kindness, practice generosity, and place Christ at the forefront of all endeavors. Remember, I am always here to share your triumphs and support you through challenges, no matter the hour. Nothing you can say or do would prevent me from standing by you, cheering you on, or picking you up when life gets tough.

Thank you for being my greatest teachers, for forgiving my mistakes, for the grace you extend to me, and for the joy of being not just your mother but your friend. Our little world together is my most treasured possession.

With all my love and more,

Momma

My Family
September 2023

Momma,

There are moments in life that are imprinted on our hearts forever; special memories that, when recalled, allow us to relive the warmth and joy all over again. Every Black Friday shopping spree, the first time you held your grandchildren, the afternoons spent mowing the lawn and soaking in the serene beauty of the pond - these are moments that have woven the colorful tapestry of our lives together. Celebrating my successes with you, feeling the weight of your pride and love through a simple hug, reminded me of the profound bond we share. As well as the tears you'd wipe when failures felt larger than life, when it was hard to stand you were there.

Through every chapter of our lives, you've been the embodiment of resilience. Your laugh, the radiance of your smile, the comfort of your embraces, and the tender touch of your hands have been my sanctuary. I cherish the warmth that enveloped me whenever you wrapped me in a towel after a swim, or how you'd gently caress my head when I was sick. More than anything, your unwavering faith and loving heart have been my guideposts.

It wasn't until I matured that I fully grasped the depth of adversity you've faced, the pain and trauma you've endured. My heart ached with the realization that healing seemed an elusive dream for you. Yet, witnessing the transformation in you over these past few years has been a gift. Indeed, we may challenge each other, our opinions might diverge, and our paths might take different turns, but at the core of it all, you are more than just my mother - you are my friend, my anchor, and for that, I am eternally grateful.

I often see a reflection of Nanny in yourself, but with an extra dash of feistiness. Watching you care for your brothers, and seeing the devotion with which you tended to your dad the last years of his life, your strength and compassion shine brightly. It's these qualities that evoke the deepest emotions, not just in me, but in everyone whose lives you touch.

You've often expressed regrets, apologized for the choices made, the hardships we faced, and the lapses along the way. With this letter, and through every word in this book, I hope to reassure you that despite the tumultuous path we've walked, it's the steps we take forward that truly define us. The divine spectacle of healing unfolding in your life is a prayer answered, a yearning fulfilled.

Momma, in the last few years as you encountered a new chapter of true self-love, I told you that it's time to forgive yourself, to love yourself unreservedly, and to surrender to the healing touch of grace each day brings. Our journeys are entwined with moments of pain and beauty, but it's through these experiences we grow, we learn, and ultimately, we find redemption. It is possible.

Always remember, no matter the challenges, the disagreements, or the trials we've faced, at the end of the day, you are my mom, my light, my hero. Thank you for being you—imperfect, beautiful, and absolutely irreplaceable. And momma, you are enough.

With all my love and endless gratitude,

-Misty "Hope"

Summer,

In the quiet moments when I sit to reflect on the myriad of blessings in my life, your name etches itself across my heart with a permanence reserved for the most treasured memories and impactful presences. Today, as I pen down my thoughts, I find myself bathed in gratitude for you - not just as my sister but as the embodiment of love, resilience, and unyielding support that you have been to me and to all whose lives you touch.

Your heart, a boundless ocean of love, the best kind of humor, and an unwavering passion for others, reminds me so much of Nanny. It's as if she left a piece of her spirit with us through you. For this, and for all the moments when your presence has been a blessing and a testament to unconditional love, I thank you.

Your laugh is a melody that lightens the darkest days, a reminder of the joy that permeates life's complexities. Your wit, sharp and sparkling, never fails to bring a smile to my face, making every conversation a treasure trove of mirth and insight. And, above all, your ability to keep me grounded, to remind me of what truly matters when life's tempests threaten to carry me away, is a gift I hold dear.

Reflecting on our shared past, I am drawn to the countless ways you've enriched my life. You've taught me acceptance with a grace that only you could. Your steadfast support and belief in me have never wavered, not even in the face of my own doubts. You were, and remain, my rock.

Thank you for the role you've played in raising me, not out of obligation, but from a place of profound love and selflessness. Your acceptance, your love, and your ability to be my steadfast guide are gifts I could never repay. Your contribution to helping me launch my business - and standing beside me as it grew into what it is today - has been instrumental in my success. Even in this professional realm, your influence shines brightly, a beacon of solidarity and support.

But perhaps, more poignant than any other aspect, is your love for my children. In loving them as your own, you've given them, and me, something truly special - an extension of your big-heartedness and generosity, a nurturing force that transcends the mere ties of blood.

In overcoming your own traumas and navigating the intricate dance of discovery towards becoming the incredible mom, wife, sister, daughter, and friend you are today, you exemplify strength and resilience. Your story is one of triumph, not because you were unscathed by the battles you've faced, but because you emerged with kindness, wisdom, and love intact.

It's impossible to articulate the depth of my gratitude and admiration for you. Words seem woefully inadequate to encapsulate the expanse of what you mean to me and to those lucky enough to know you. Yet, I hope in these words you find a reflection of the love and esteem in which I hold you, a mirror to the beauty of your soul as perceived through my eyes.

Thank you, Summer, for being my unyielding support, my confidante, my teacher, and above all, my beloved sister.

I love you so much.

- Hopey

Me, Momma & Summer
May 2023

Thank You

To My Beloved Family and Cherished Individuals in My Life,

From the deepest recess of my heart, I write this letter to express a magnitude of gratitude that words can scarcely encapsulate. This memoir, a mosaic of my life's moments, is incomplete without acknowledging the vibrant threads each of you have woven into the fabric of my being.

Thank you to my beloved in-laws, whose love has never felt anything short of genuine parental affection. Your unwavering support, the joyous echoes of laughter with our children amidst the family farm, and every cherished memory in between are treasures to my soul. Thank you for the sanctuary of love and affection you have invariably provided. To John & Ash, thank you for your friendship and the many trips, some still to come, packed with unforgettable memories and tons of fun, as they have truly enriched my life.

Being an aunt is a title I wear with indescribable pride. To my nephews and niece, each of you has enriched my life with pure acceptance and affection. Caden, from our playful times in your infancy to witnessing the exceptional young man you've become, know you are cherished beyond measure. Your laugh and humor envelop me and make me live in the present. Our trip to Las Vegas will be something I will cherish forever.

Peyton, your enormous heart and infectious smile fill my soul. The day you were born, I found out I was pregnant with Braylee, and as I gazed down at you, I couldn't help but wonder about the person you'd become as we watched you grow up with our own children. I'm really proud of the man you've become. You are wise and considerate, and I'm excited for your future. Also, your laugh is one of my favorite things.

Grayson, my lil sidekick, your unique essence and humor have undoubtedly kept me laughing and focused on the light-hearted gift of life. You have uplifted my heart through some of my most challenging seasons, always making me feel loved and appreciated. Every moment with you is pure entertainment and I hope you know how much I cherish each one.

Laken, your distinctiveness, wit, and love for the Lord inspire me daily; you are a gift of unparalleled worth. I never know what will come out of your mouth, whether a wise statement or the best comeback; I'm grateful to know you and watch you blossom into the amazing young woman God created you to be. Remember, you are enough. Always.

To my son from another mother - Burton, your presence in my life was unexpected but a gift. Watching you grow, evolve, and step into the young man God has called you to be has been and will continue to be something I'm thankful for. Your genuine heart, work ethic, and sincerity are truly an inspiration. I am eternally grateful for this and for the privilege of considering you a son of my own. Thanks for keeping me laughing.

Paul, thank you for the life and love you've given my sister. Your unwavering kindness and sincerity are appreciated for sticking by us through some of the most challenging situations and trials. Our many beach trips, late-night stops for food, and your childhood stories are memories I'll forever cherish.

Teresa, you have loved me as your own, the warmth you've extended to my children, and the new dimensions of joy you brought to our Christmases. Jenna and Karlee (and the guys), the vibrancy of life you've instilled in us through your stories, laughter, and love has been a blessing beyond words.

To my departed grandparents, all four now residing in Heaven, I want you to know that you are deeply missed. Your impact on my life has been profound, and I cherish the memories I hold close to my heart. Whenever I spot a bird resting nearby, I can't help but wonder if it's your spirit visiting me. Your most valuable lesson was that God is my ultimate source of strength and fulfillment. Thank you for everything.

To my grandparents, whom I inherited through the gift of marriage, I express my deep gratitude for your unwavering love, generosity, and gentle spirits. Grandpa Crey, you were the rock of my husband's life, and your absence is keenly felt each day. Although a piece of my husband's soul departed with you, I am thankful for the invaluable lessons and immense kindness you imparted to him. Your legacy lives on through him, carrying forward your cherished memories, laughter, and teachings. I hope you look down with pride on the legacy Ryan continues to uphold.

Joycie, I appreciate you for being like a second mom to me throughout these years. Thank you for constantly checking in, creating enjoyable moments for us, and being a consistent presence in our lives. You are the kind of friend everyone needs.

Jarrod, you truly make me feel special whenever I walk into a room. Your friendship is invaluable to me, and I appreciate how our lives are connected. Thank you for including me in your experiences, making every trip beyond epic, and sharing your family with me. You mean a lot to me, my friend.

Mr. Murphy, my guiding light through the storms of childhood, your office was not just a refuge but a sanctuary where *creativity and kindness knew no bounds. The koala you gifted me will forever symbolize the generosity and safety I felt in your presence.*

Amy, your support was crucial in bringing this book to life. Though occasionally annoying, your unwavering belief in me and the gentle nudge toward accountability was truly valued. Your laughter, love, and friendship are treasures I sometimes feel unworthy of. Your soul is precious, and your profound impact on me is beyond words.

Jessica, I am grateful for our conversation on the beach that day. Your words profoundly impacted me, and I believe it was a moment orchestrated by God. You helped unlock the next chapter of my journey, and I am truly grateful for that.

Cindy and Scott, words can't capture the depth of gratitude I hold for you. You've witnessed my family and me evolve, and through your unwavering faith, inspiration, and courage to pursue your calling, I discovered mine. Your steadfast friendship and mentorship have been invaluable in shaping my life. Thank you for everything.

David, you've evolved into a cherished friend and mentor, a bond I hold dear. Your unique kindness and unparalleled compassion towards others are truly exceptional. I sincerely appreciate your friendship, acceptance, and guidance.

Mark, in full transparency, I was hoping Angi was my coach that day. I was a little worried your energy was a bit too much for me. Little did I know you'd be a perfect fit, continue to coach me for nearly 10 years, and become a lifelong friend. There isn't a season of my business you didn't hold my hand through, and I'm grateful for you and your precious family. Thanks for kicking me in the rear and for always being real.

To 1001 - I love having you in my corner. Thanks for paving the way for the rest of us.

Julie, thank you for asking. Thank you for the gift of opportunity you sincerely offered to me that day in 2007 and for cheering me on all these years.

Angi, I couldn't have made the shift in my journey without your leadership and friendship. You inspire me to be better in many ways, and I'm eternally grateful for the influence of your leadership, heart, and love for others. Thank you for believing in me, challenging me, and leading me.

Ryno, my taco-loving friend, you have become one of my best friends over the last two years, and I love being able to share this corporate journey with you. You have become a mentor, a guide, and a partner, and I can't thank you enough for guiding me through the seasons of learning and inspiring me to show up better each day.

Gloria, from hair to therapy, you cover it all. Thank you for your support, your love, and for cheering me on. Your family means so much to me, and I'm grateful and truly honored to call you a friend.

To my extended family, my amazing aunts/uncles, cousins, friends, and every soul who has left an indelible mark on my heart, your influences have shaped me in profound ways. I am deeply thankful to those who have stood by me through thick and thin, whose silence-breaking outreach and unwavering support have been my lifeline.

To my childhood pastor's family, Beacon of Hope team, mentors, colleagues, coaches, and my youth group, your belief, support, and guiding light have been pivotal to my path to healing, discovery, and fulfillment.

This memoir chronicles my life and is a testament to the love, inspiration, and guidance each of you has bestowed upon me. Saying "thank you" feels inadequate when I reflect on the immeasurable impact you've all had on my life. Yet, with a heart brimming with gratitude, I say, with all my love, thank you.

Forever grateful,

Hope

Thank you, dear readers, for choosing to walk this path with me through the pages of my memoir. Your support illuminates the narrative of our shared humanity, fostering a connection that transcends the written word. I am profoundly grateful for your willingness to explore the depths of my experiences, understanding that within them, we uncover universal truths about love, loss, and the resilience of the human spirit. Your engagement and reflections are invaluable, turning this personal voyage into a collective expedition. Thank you for being an integral part of my continued story.

- Hope Shortt